Swachh Indore

Swachh Indore

(How Indore became the cleanest city in India?)

P. Narahari, IAS

PRABHAT PAPERBACKS

Published by
PRABHAT PAPERBACKS
An imprint of Prabhat Prakashan Pvt. Ltd.
4/19 Asaf Ali Road,
New Delhi-110002 (INDIA)
e-mail: prabhatbooks@gmail.com

ISBN 978-93-5521-324-2
SWACHH INDORE
by Shri P. Narahari, IAS

Edition
First, 2022

Price
₹ 300.00 (Rupees Three Hundred only)

Printed at
R-Tech Offset Printers, Delhi

"India has been making steady progress in its vision to become 'Swachh Bharat'. Such a movement calls for successful participation from all stakeholders of our society. Different parts of India are at varying stages of the 'Swachhta' journey, and there is something to learn from everyone. 'Swachh Indore' is one such story which can encourage meaningful conversations about the role all of us can play in civic movements."

—Sachin Tendulkar

This book is dedicated to
all the
safai karmacharis
(sanitation workers) of Indore.

Preface

The city of Indore has done something which in Indian conditions is unimaginable. It took months for many to realise and come to terms whether it is true. Is Indore really that clean? Is it still that clean city now also? How can a north Indian city be cleaner than Mysore, a south Indian city? Who made such a thing happened? Will it sustain to be the cleanest city of the country and for how long?

What are the strategies that enabled Indore to be numero uno city in the country? How different are the strategies that are making even foreign delegates come to Indore to see its success story? Can this success story be replicated in any other part of the country or in other countries?

Who are the officers, public representatives and civic societies that worked smartly and differently from routine and enabled such an enviable story to be written?

How did one *swachhta* song become an anthem for the residents of Indore to wake up and make their city the cleanest in India? Is it that that motivational song that it swayed the way for Indore to become the cleanest city in the country?

How the success story of Indore has revolutionised the entire *swachhta* work in the country? How it is an inspiration for other cities to follow the success story of Indore? Why are other cities not able to compete and dethrone Indore as the number one city?

After the initial few months of campaign how there was massive reduction of vector borne diseases in Indore? How a cascading effect of Swacchta enabled cleaning of one of the dirtiest Rivers-Kahn? How the cleanliness led to the dumping yard become a favourite Tea spot for Indoris? How women leadership made this campaign one of the most sustainable models of sanitation? How cleanliness has enabled attract businesses and other opportunities to Indore?

All these questions need to be answered. And this book answers all such questions and sets aside all such doubts about cleanliness of Indore. The amazing journey of Indore from 2016 till date is detailed in this book. Wish the readers find it an interesting study and like it as well.

Ram Navami, 2022 **—Parikipandla Narahari, IAS**
Bhopal

Acknowledgements

The journey of Indore wouldn't have been possible if Asheesh Singh, IAS, the then CEO Zila Panchayat of Indore hadn't taken keen interest in the *Swachh Bharat* Rural programme. His enthusiasm made me pool in all the experience and resources and work for achieving the set goal. Smt Kavita Patidar, the then Chairperson of *Zila Panchayat* actively worked with the team and spearheaded the programme in all the villages. She took along all the other public representatives in this special programme.

When we started the SBM Urban in Indore city, it was Manish Singh, the then Municipal Commissioner and Mrs. Malini Gaud, the then Mayor who wholeheartedly put all their efforts and galvanised the entire city for taking it to number one position. The then Member of Parliament from Indore and Speaker of Lok Sabha Smt Sumitra Mahajan was the first citizen of Indore to hold broom for cleaning up Indore. Their contribution can't be recognised in words. Together as a team, we were able to share our responsibilities and achieve this stupendous task.

I have to thank the Hon'ble Chief Minister of Madhya Pradesh Shri Shivraj Singh Chauhan for reposing faith in me to lead the district and support me at all times for achieving these results. He came to Indore whenever requested to acknowledge the work done by the entire administration.

Special thanks to Hon'ble Shri Venkaiah Naidu, the then Minister of Housing and Urban Poverty Alleviation, Urban Development who always supported every little effort made by Indore and never forgot to mention Indore in all his SBM meetings in the country. I learnt many things from him when I accompanied him as a part of the delegation to Germany in 2016. His statesman qualities are worth mentioning which I am in awe of.

I need to thank Nilesh Dube, Deputy Mission Director of Swachh Bharat Mission (Urban) at the Directorate of Urban Administration, Bhopal from whom I learnt how SBM has to be managed at state level. He single-handedly spearheaded the SBM programme in the state ever since its inception. I have to thank Shuriah Niyazi for the data collection and in helping me drafting this document. Special mention of Sanjeev Parsai is essential for helping me in finalising this document.

I need to thank Media of Indore for being the spokesperson of all the good efforts made by the administration in making Indore cleanest city. Their valuable inputs and also showing the mirror helped up achieve this stupendous achievement.

I need to wholeheartedly thank all the *safai karmacharis* of Indore for scripting such a story for Indore and make many cities to follow their footsteps. I thank all the persons for allowing to be interviewed and express their views and making this book see the light of the day. I have to thank all my seniors and my supporting staff for the solid support and guidance in all my works.

I have to thank my family members for being the pillars of support throughout my 20 years of administrative journey and enabling to me to try my crazy ideas and succeed.

Contents

1

Background of Indore

Indore is the largest city in the state of Madhya Pradesh. According to the 2011 census, it has a population of 21,67,447 that inhabits just 530 square km. It is also the most densely populated city in Madhya Pradesh.

Indore comes under Tier-2 cities in India. The Indore metropolitan area, comprising its urban and surrounding areas, has the highest population in the state, with 21 lakh people. It serves as the headquarters of both the Indore district and Indore division. It is also called the commercial capital of the state of Madhya Pradesh. Besides, the city is famous as a centre of education in Madhya Pradesh and across the country. Before India became independent, it was the capital of the princely state of Indore. Indore city, located at the southern end of the Malwa plateau, is 190 km west of the state capital Bhopal.

Shortly after India gained independence in 1947, this princely state acceded to the Indian Union along with other neighbouring princely states. With the formation of Central India in 1948, Indore became the summer capital of the state. But with the formation of the state of Madhya Pradesh on 1st November, 1956, the capital was shifted to Bhopal. Indore has transformed from a traditional commercial urban centre into a modern dynamic commercial capital of the state.

Indore was established as a trade market on the Narmada River valley route leading from Ujjain to Omkareshwar. At the same time, the Indreshwar Temple was constructed in 1741, and Indore was derived from the name Indur. During the Maratha period, Bajirao Peshwa gained authority over the region and made his commander Malhar Rao Holkar the *zamindar* (landlord) of the area who laid the foundation of the Holkar dynasty. The reign of the Holkar dynasty lasted until India became independent. Indore was also the British Central India Agency's summer capital and that of Central India (1948–56) before merging with Madhya Pradesh. The Krishnapura Chhatris, built on the banks of the Kahn River, are dedicated to the Holkar rulers.

Indore is located in the western region of Madhya Pradesh at the southern edge of the Malwa plateau. It is situated on the banks of Saraswati and Kahn rivers, the Kshipra River's tributaries and the average elevation is 553.00 meters above sea level. It is a high plateau on the south of which is the Vindhya Range. Apart from the Yashwant Lake, there are many lakes such as Sirpur Lake, Bilawali Lake, Sukhnivas Lake and Pipliyapala Lake supplying water to the city. The soil in the city area is predominantly black. In the suburbs, the soil is largely red and black. The underlying rocks of the area are composed of black basalt, and their acidic and basic variants go back to the Cretaceous age. This region is classified under the Seismic Zone III of India, which means an earthquake of moderate intensity having a magnitude 6.5 and above on the Richter scale can hit the region.

Tourist Attractions

Indore and its surrounding areas abound in places of tourist interest. The Ralamandal Wildlife Sanctuary in Indore houses different species of birds and animals. Home to leopard, deer, chital, blackbuck, sambar, blue bull, barking deer, wild hare, and an umpteen variety of birds, this sanctuary is nothing short of a paradise.

Janapav, also known as Janapav Kuti, is another popular tourist attraction of Indore. It is situated on the Indore-Mumbai highway, near the village of Janapav Kuti in Indore district's Mhow tehsil, about 45 km from the city of Indore.

The city also boasts of a large and well-maintained zoo known as Kamla Nehru Prani Sangrahalaya, where one can see many beautiful birds and animals. Other famous places in Indore include Khajrana Ganesh Temple, Lal Bagh, Kanch Mandir, Rajwada, among others.

Connectivity

Indore is well connected to the rest of the country by road, rail and air. Indore is also well connected to major Indian cities like Varanasi, Delhi, Lucknow, Bhopal, Hyderabad and Kolkata by air and it is also an international cargo hub. The Devi Ahilyabai Holkar International Airport is the busiest in the state, and the new makeover of the airport has given it the International tag.

Indore is also well connected by rail to all major cities of India. Besides, a good network of roadways connects Indore well with the rest of the country. Regular bus services for Indore are available from nearby cities.

Cuisine

Indore has twice made it to the Guinness Book of World Records for its amazing food and cuisine. It was included for the largest tea party in the world and for making the world's largest burger.

If we talk about places in India and their famous cuisines, Indore is a leader among them. Indore is famous for its extensive food and dishes. The city is famed for its variety of mouth-watering items like *kachori, samosa, gajak, sev-parmal*, sago *khichdi, chaat*, a wide variety of *namkeen, poha, bhel, panipuri*, hot dog, egg banjo, *moong bhajiya, dahi vada, sabudana vada* and they are all famous for their distinctive taste. Among the mouth-watering and lip-smacking desserts and sweets of Indore are *moongdaal halwa, gajar halwa, rabri, malpua, faluda kulfi, gulab jamun, rasmalai, rasgulla, imarti*. Indore has many other traditional sweets on its menu that are finger-licking delicacies.

One can relish various exotic dishes, including Mughlai, Bengali, Maratha, Rajasthani dishes, and various local dishes like *Dal-Bafla*, which are quite famous and available in many restaurants. Food lovers make it a point to visit Sarafa Bazar and Chhappan Dukan, where many restaurants and food joints are located. Generally, *namkeen* is served prominently in Indore. *Sev-Parmal* is a popular snack here which is a speciality of Malwa. Recently, several famous chain restaurants like McDonald's, Domino's, Pizza Hut, KFC, Subway, Barista Lavazza and Cafe Coffee Day have opened their branches in Indore.

Industries in Indore

Indore is a commercial centre for goods and services. Indore's gross domestic product in 2011 was $ 14 billion (Data Source to be quoted). The city has attracted investors from many countries at the Global Investors Summits. The Indore grain market is the central market of the Indore division. It is the country's main marketing centre for soybean. Besides wheat, gram, dollar gram, all kinds of pulses, cotton and all other crops are traded here. Farmers of nearby districts like Dhar, Khargone, Ujjain, Dewas etc., are also connected to the Indore grain market.

It is noteworthy that since the British era, Indore has

developed as an industrial city. Over 5,000 small-scale industries are located here. Pithampur is a well-known industrial town of Madhya Pradesh, situated very close to Indore. Pithampur hosts a large number of pharmaceutical, vehicle and automotive industries. It is also known as the 'Detroit of India'. Over 650 small scale industries and over 150 medium and large-scale industrial units are operating in Pithampur. It employs about 30,000 people. Automobile giants have set up their units here. Exports from Pithampur Special Economic Zone have been on the rise. The Madhya Pradesh Stock Exchange, India's third oldest stock market, is located in Indore.

Education

Apart from being an industrial city, Indore has also emerged as a centre of education. It is the only city in India where both the Indian Institute of Management (IIM, Indore) and the Indian Institute of Technology (IIT, Indore) are established. These educational institutions are known to provide a well-rounded education to students. That is why Indore has emerged as one of the leading education hubs of India.

Indore is home to many schools, colleges and universities. The schools are equipped with excellent teaching staff that provide quality education to the students. Indore has a large student population and is a major educational centre in central India. Most of the primary and secondary schools in Indore are recognized by the Central Board of Secondary Education (CBSE). However, a considerable number of schools are affiliated with the ICSE

Board, NIOS Board, Chhattisgarh Board and State Level MP Board.

Daly College, founded in 1882 by Sir Henry Daly of the British Indian Army during India's colonial British Raj, is one of the oldest co-educational boarding schools in the world, and follows an English public school model. It is a co-educational residential and day boarding school affiliated to the CBSE, and today imparts education to more than 2,000 students. The alumni council consists of some members of the royal families of India.

The Holkar Science College is recognized as a model college by the Government of Madhya Pradesh. It is an autonomous college and offers courses at UG and PG level in Science and Computer Applications streams.

The Indore School of Social Work was founded in 1951 and is dedicated to excellence in its teaching, research and professional practice in Social Work and works in both the field of education and research. It has been providing training to professional social workers since 1951.

The Devi Ahilya Vishwavidyalaya (or DAVV, formerly known as Indore University) in Indore has nearly 300 affiliated colleges operating under its aegis in addition to the University teaching departments and centres. It has two campuses within the city, one at the Takshila range (near the Bhawarkua intersection) and the other at Rabindra Nath Tagore Road, Indore. DAVV offers undergraduate courses, Integrated MBA, Integrated M.Tech., postgraduate and doctoral courses in various areas such as engineering, business, law, etc. DAVV is accredited by the National Assessment and Accreditation Council (NAAC). The university's jurisdiction extends to seven tribal-dominated rural districts of Indore, namely, Khargone, Khandwa, Alirajpur, Dhar, Jhabua, Burhanpur and Barwani. The university has about 9,000 students on its campus and over 3,00,000 students in affiliated colleges. DAVV serves over 3,00,000 students every year through well-qualified human resources, with a diversified course structure, inter-disciplinary research and value-based education. The Institute of Engineering and Technology, DAVV, has been operating since 1996 and now offers several B.E. and M.E. courses.

Mahatma Gandhi Memorial Medical College is another old institution, which was formerly known as King Edward Medical College. The Shri Govindram Seksaria Institute of Technology and Science was established in 1952. The headquarters of Digital Gurukul is also in Indore.

Sports

Cricket is one of the most popular sports in the city. Indore is home to the Madhya Pradesh Cricket Association, Madhya Pradesh Table Tennis Association and the Holkar Cricket Stadium, an international cricket ground situated at Race Course Road in the city, where all international and national cricket matches are held. . For the first time in the state, a cricket ODI match was played on this cricket ground. Besides, the Jawaharlal Nehru Stadium has a seating capacity of 25,000 people and is a multi-purpose stadium where many sports activities take place, including cricket, basketball, football, etc.

Besides traditional sports, there are several amazing

adventure sports, especially water sports, which tourists can enjoy in Indore at several locations. Jet skiing is one of the most thrilling of these. Tourists enjoy adventurous water sports at Choral Dam in Indore, while Hanumantiya Island is the best place for parasailing.

The sports clubs in Indore provide excellent sporting facilities to players and youngsters. Some of the famous sports clubs of Indore are the MP Cricket Association, Basketball Club, Indore, Yashwant Club, Sayaji Club, City Gymkhana, Hill Club and Saaj Club.

Indore is also a traditional centre for basketball and is home to India's first National Basketball Academy with a square indoor basketball stadium. Various national basketball championships have been successfully organised in Indore. The major sports stadiums include:

Basketball—Basketball Complex, Basketball Club

Cricket—Holkar Cricket Stadium, Jawaharlal Nehru Stadium, Khalsa School Stadium, Maharaja School Stadium

Lawn Tennis—Indore Tennis Club, Indore Residency Club

Table Tennis—Nehru Stadium TT Hall, Abhay Khel Prashal

Kabaddi—Lucky Wanderers

Chess—SKM Chess Academy, Chess Academy

Diving—Nehru Park

Media

There are 20 Hindi dailies, 7 English dailies, 24 weeklies and monthlies, 4 quarterlies, 2 bi-monthly magazines, one annual paper, and one monthly Hindi language educational newspaper named 'Campus Diary' are published from the city. Major Hindi newspapers and national media houses have their regional offices in Indore. Offices of all major news channels are also situated here.

Indore Smart City

Indore is one of the cities that were chosen in the first top 20 Smart cities. Indore Smart City is up and coming as an urban ecosystem that strives to incorporate digital technology, knowledge and resources, perk up city services, develop into a more amenable place to residents and make the city more attractive than it already is.

□

2
My Experiences

It was April 2015 when I joined as Indore Collector. The *Swachh Bharat* campaign was launched on 2ndOctober, 2014, by Prime Minister Narendra Modi. By that time, the Government of Madhya Pradesh had begun a campaign to make every district of the state Open Defecation Free (ODF) under the *Swachh Bharat* Mission *Gramin*. We have two *Swachh Bharat* Missions: one is for rural areas and the other for urban areas.

It all started from the rural areas. Indore is divided into the Zila Parishad area, which is rural, and the main city area is urban. When we began this work, we focused on the rural part to make it ODF. At that time, Asheesh Singh was the Chief Executive Officer (CEO) at Zila Panchayat.

In a briefing, he informed me that strict instructions were received from the government that we had to make the rural area open defecation free after Nadia District of West Bengal had done so. He said that we had to start this campaign at the earliest on the instructions of the state government. We therefore decided to start this by organising a meeting. We invited the chairman of the Zila Panchayat Smt. Kavita Patidar and its members, *janpad* members, and the *sarpanch* at the Indore collectorate.

We informed them that they should be ready to accept this challenge and had to make every effort to make rural areas ODF. Everyone present at the meeting took the oath and then began the work. Those 8 months of sheer hard work of those involved made us succeed in making Indore rural district open defecation free.

We began our work in April 2015 and achieved our goal on 26th January, 2016. And this was a very important achievement as Indore rural became the second rural district in the entire country to become open defecation free. This milestone made Indore a sensation in the entire country. It was a real achievement for all those involved.

Chief Minister Shivraj Singh Chouhan was invited to Indore to officially declare the area ODF. He praised the efforts of the entire district administration. He also said that Indore had become an example for all the districts to follow. This feat of Indore came as a surprise to everyone. The Government of India also called us to know about the measures we had taken and how we managed to do it in such a short span. We explained our measures through a presentation to the government.

At that time, rural areas had a population of about 11 lakhs. In terms of percentage, this is about 1/3rd of the total population of the whole district. We achieved this feat with the help of government officials, public representatives and the people.

The fourth sector to help us was the media, which was always available for the city's sake. I always give importance to all four of them for this achievement. And I feel that if you do not include these stakeholders, you cannot succeed in any public campaign. It was not just a campaign by a Collector or Chief Executive Officer (CEO) of the Zila Panchayat but the contribution of the common people and lower-rung staff of different government organisations involved in the campaign.

I worked as collector for 10 years, and before that, was CEO at the Zila Panchayat of Chhindwara district as well. I had thus a field experience of more than 10 to 11 years. I saw different kinds of programmes related to *swachhata* (sanitation), like the Total Sanitation Campaign (TSC), *Nirmal Bharat Abhiyan*, and finally saw this *Swachh Bharat* campaign. I had also worked on similar campaigns earlier, but they weren't as successful.

We attained success this time because of the deliberations and change in the campaign strategies and then decided to bring about a behavioural change. We believed that it is behavioural change that matters most in sanitation campaigns.

Normally, the administration focuses on people to build toilets and hopes that behavioural change will follow. But that is not correct. We have to first bring behavioural change, and then toilets should be built. Hence, our concept this time was not actually about construction of toilets; it was majorly a concept of behavioural change.

Almost every morning at four o'clock, I used to visit villages in any one of the blocks in the district along with my officers and the media. We aimed to work at the potential sites for open defecation. We knew there were two to three specific places in every village where people would go for open defecation.

These places are usually the banks of a pond or a deserted field, or some government land full of bushes and so on. If such places were found, then our teams would go there and focus on talking to persons who were defecating there.

People generally go to open places for defecation in the mornings or in the evenings after sunset. Earlier, we tried to visit such places during office timings from 10 am to 6 pm and talk to people. But we soon realised that it was not the right time for talking about behavioural change. We realised that we should go there early in the morning when people actually go out to attend to nature's call. We then tried interacting with those people at that time. We hit the bull's eye.

In this whole exercise, the role played by the motivators was very important. All of these motivators were ordinary citizens and not government employees. They were picked by our team and trained for community works.

They took this programme into their own hands. Irrespective of whether government officials went there or not, these people would definitely stand there. We had given them proper training. They were given training on what to talk about, which would affect their psyche. It was explained to the people why they should not defecate in the open. Hence, the role played by the motivators has been very important.

Even small children played an important role in the whole campaign. We trained school boys and girls. We organised a *vanar sena* of these students. After the required training and orientation, this *vanar sena* of kids became so strict that they did not allow anyone to defecate in the open.

We particularly targeted the sites that were full of bushes and shrub growth and cleared and cleaned them. The second thing we did was to light up these sites with halogens since people seek darkness to defecate in the open.

People go out to defecate at four o'clock because it is dark at that time. We ensured that the areas where people defecate do not remain under cover of darkness. Besides, we put up small things there like religious signs etc., because when people see such things, they do not defecate at that place as it is a sacred place.

These kinds of things were done so that people would not defecate there. The whole effort was geared to making people agree with and support the measures being undertaken by us. The children who were there had poles and sticks in their hands, which they used to hit the *lota* or the pot that people used to carry with them.

The idea was that if grown-ups do such things, then those defecating in the open would quarrel with them, but it was not easy to fight with children because they are children.

I being the Collector, Zila Panchayat CEO or President Zila Panchayat, would go there at four in the morning most of the time. Whenever the senior government officers used to go for their morning rounds, they used to take the media with them so that the media would also know what we were doing. The media also focused on the innovative ideas adopted by the administration for a positive purpose.

The best things were shown to the media, who helped people understand what was bad. The media supported a lot. The special thing about this programme and its strategy was to change the place of defecation from an open defecation site to the person's residence or his/her household.

Earlier, the focus of the campaign was on building more toilets. But even after toilets were built, the old habit of defecating in the open did not go easily. People used to go out to defecate, although there was a toilet in the house. We focused on sending them back home from the open defecation site. People were told to either construct a toilet at home or use a public toilet. This strategy was very successful. That is why we achieved so much success in a short time. We were the finalists for the Prime Minister's award for excellence for the amazing work done in making Indore rural district open defecation free. We were also among the five districts that were selected from all over the country. We eventually secured the number two position in the country. Our strategy has been appreciated throughout the country.

After our success in the rural area, we then moved to the urban area. When the work in rural areas was going on, the urban administration department too started its campaign.

Manish Singh was then the Municipal Commissioner of Indore, and the Mayor was Malini Gaud. We held a meeting with them and informed them that rural area had become open defecation free, and now we had to try and make urban areas too open defecation free. Manish Singh organised a workshop for all the corporators.

In the workshop, we invited motivators, the *sarpanches* of gram panchayats involved in making rural areas open defecation free. There they were briefed on how the rural area was made ODF and how it is being sustained. It usually happens that after declaring ODF, nothing changes, but in this case, we had focused on behavioural change.

After Manish Singh took up the initiative in urban areas in March 2016, the Government of India declared the ranking of cities in which Indore stood 25th city in the country and Mysore obtained the top position for being the cleanest city.

We conducted this workshop and then adopted the same strategy to involve government officials, public representatives, the public and the media. We also decided how we ought to run this campaign.

The campaign was started with a door-to-door collection of household waste. We then started working on making the city open defecation free. The municipal commissioner identified all the open defecation places in line with what we had done in the rural areas.

We talked to the people and asked them as to why they defecated in the open. Their answer was either they did not have toilets, or even after having toilets, they had some behavioural issues. Or, they had a water problem. In slums, they do not have adequate space. We then constructed public toilets.

As far as the concept of door-to-door household waste collection is concerned, it is the duty or basic principle of a municipal corporation in every city to collect waste, but this was not being done in almost all the municipal bodies. This was an implementation issue.

Every municipal corporation should effectively do it. The methodology for this has been given in the guidelines of the *Swachh Bharat* Mission.

Segregation of waste has to be done. Door-to-door collection and segregation of solid and wet waste too must be carried out. All guidelines on where they will go after segregation and how they will be disposed of scientifically with no harm to the environment were available, but implementation was not being done.

Manish Singh took it as a challenging task and started its implementation. The first step was door-to-door collection and disposal, the second was making spaces open defecation free and the third was the cleaning of the roads.

We identified all the things that were responsible for making the city look ugly. Those things being identified, we then had to find a solution for them. A system was then created for sweeping the roads. Road sweeping was divided into two ways. Sweeping had to be done according to the width of the road. Earlier, sweepers used to sweep roads of any width whether it was 6 feet, 15 feet or 30 feet.

It was decided that the sweepers would sweep those roads which were smaller in width. But for bigger roads, there would be mechanised sweeping machines. This work was started from the super corridor of Indore for which mechanised sweeping machines were used.

Machines were purchased. The Government of India's funds under the *Swachh Bharat* Mission, which the state government provided, was utilised properly by the Indore Municipal Corporation.

Imagine if we deploy a sweeper for cleaning a big road; how much time he would take to sweep that road. The aim was not to remove them but to shift them to smaller roads. This way, efficiency was increased, which was an exemplary initiative.

The next initiative was the removal of dustbins from the entire city. The city was converted into a zero-dustbin city. We observed that if there was a dustbin, it became a centre for dumping waste. Instead of depositing the waste inside the dustbin, they would spoil the nearby areas by throwing waste here and there. And in the absence of daily collection, it becomes a nightmare for the city. In the successful campaign in Indore, one cannot find dustbins. Under this campaign, sanitation workers collect waste from your home, office, organisation or firm directly thus minimising the need for throwing it in the open.

The door-to-door collection was made efficient in the city. Hence, there has been no need for dustbins. Soon, because of Indore becoming a dustbin-free city, we could see the changes in the entire city almost immediately.

The other important thing is citizen engagement. That was the most important thing that has happened during this project. Meanwhile, a smart city campaign was also launched under which 100 smart cities had to be selected through a competitive process.

Citizen engagement played a major role in Indore being selected among 100 smart cities because it was a point-based system. A competitive environment was created by the Government of India for choosing the smart cities and citizens were involved in the project. The media and social media were used in a big way during the selection process.

The common people were invited to tell how a smart city could become a reality. What were the issues that needed to be addressed to make the city a smart city? We ran a year-long citizen engagement campaign in which municipal corporation and the Citizen groups (Indian medical associations, lawyers' associations, teachers' associations, resident welfare associations) were all involved.

All stakeholders were involved in the project. We also initiated a parallel campaign to involve these people in an awareness drive. The involvement of audio-visual media was another initiative undertaken by us. We composed a song in order to create a feeling that the city must remain clean.

The first song that was designed was *'ho halla.'"* We involved audio-visuals in these campaigns because of the impact that it made on the citizens. During my childhood, when we used to go for outdoor activities like scouts and guides, we used to be woken up in the morning through songs.

There was a song in Hindi: *'Uth Jaag Musafir Bhor Bhaye, Ab Rain Kahan Jo Sowat Hai| Jo Sowat Hai So Khowat Hai, Jo Jagat Hai So Pawat Hai'.* This song motivated us to get up early and start our activities ASAP.

It has always been my belief that whether it is the *bhajans* in a temple or the '*azaan*' of a mosque, they all help to create an environment. This motivates us to do something good in the morning.

I always felt that there should be a song which motivates the people and tells them that their city should be clean. It should be a matter of joy to all of them that their city should climb up to the top position from Number 25. Created by Hrishikesh Pandey, Bollywood Singer Shaan sang this song '*Ho Halla*', and in the mornings, the garbage vehicle that went to collect garbage played this melodious song to wake up the citizens. On the one hand, it not only announced to the people that the garbage vehicle had arrived, and they had to hand over the garbage but it was also a reminder that they had to make their city number one; not only reach the top place but also maintain it.

This song also served as a motivation for the sanitation workers of the city. Earlier, the vehicles which used to collect waste were not regular. They used to do their rounds only for a few days in a week. But this time, it was totally different. They had to go to the designated places every day.

Our first song *'Ho Halla'* became very popular. Indore is number one because of everyone's hard work. First, it was *'Ho Halla'*, the second song was *'Hai Halla'*, and the third was *'Hattrick Lagayenge.'* And for the fourth year, the song was *'Chauka Lagayenge.'* I was involved in all the four years of making of these songs and "Swachchta ka panch" for the fifth-year campaign.

In July 2017, I joined at Bhopal as the Commissioner of Public Relations Department, and then later became the Urban Administration Commissioner in June 2019. I ran the campaign for *Swachh Survekshan* 2020 for the whole of MP. The audio-visual medium made a lot of impact in all the cities of Madhya Pradesh.

I remember it was in 2017 that a cricket match was organised. Along with MPCA officials, we had decided that we had to clean the stadium in just an hour both from inside and outside. And we did it. These are the things which make an impact on people. We had heard about Japan. They went to play the World Cup football championship in South Africa but lost badly.

Everyone had left the stadium, but the Japanese spectators who went to watch the game remained there and cleaned the whole stadium. Only then did they leave the stadium. What made news was the cleanliness of Japanese spectators, not their defeat.

This inculcation in small children, adults, and all age groups has to become a part of life. This is what behavioural change means. Behavioural change has to be everywhere and, in every person, and has to be there every time, not at any particular time.

In 2018, I made a song for the state for the first time, my effort being to make the whole state clean. We made songs for the whole state in 2018, 2019 and 2020. I also made a similar song for Bhopal City, when I joined in June 2019 as urban administration commissioner and remained there till July 2020. During this period, we designed *Swachhta* programmes for 100 urban local bodies. We managed to put 7 cities from Madhya Pradesh in the Top 100 cities of India.

In 2020, we had planned that at least 20 cities from the state should come up in the Top 100, which finally happened. Bhopal came in the top 10. It slipped in 2019 to 20th place but then made a comeback in 2020.

The main thrust of the campaign was the door-to-door collection of garbage. We focused on 100 cities of the state out of 376 towns. After selecting 100 towns, we implemented a focused approach where we planned to adopt the Indore model.

Our effort involved organising meetings in almost all the bigger municipal corporations of the state. Other than meetings, we also extensively toured these areas. We discussed the deficiencies that these cities had, what was not happening and how to address those things.

We then held divisional level meetings to identify targeted areas and what needed to be done, including motivating the staff. We did everything possible to achieve the set targets. Then again, the successful formula of government officials, public representatives, public and media was utilised in the campaign. These efforts not only enabled to achieve the set targets in *Swachhta Survekshan* 2020 but also in 2021.

□

3

The Journey of Indore towards being a Cleanest City

A person who had come for the *darshan* of Indore's Khajrana Ganesh Temple casually threw away some peanut shells. After about two minutes, two young men walking along that path picked up the shells and dumped them in the dustbin. The youths told the person to always put the garbage in the dustbin and not make the city dirty. The young men were not from any cleaning agency; they were also visiting Indore city for *darshan*. The incident happened in the year 2018.

The person who threw the shells was testing the truth about the things he had heard about the passion of the people of Indore for cleanliness.

This feeling of cleanliness among the people of Indore did not come in a day; but it took a long time, and we can see the results now. Indore has again won the title in the *Swachh Survekshan* 2021, conducted in the country and how it managed to reclaim its number one position in cleanliness consecutively for the fifth time.

Before this, in the preceding years 2017, 18, 19, and 20 Indore had already backed the title of number one clean city by the central government. How Indore became No. 1 for the fifth consecutive time? The municipal corporation, employees and people of Indore contributed a lot towards that.

Without their cooperation, the city could not have achieved this position. Mysore received the country's cleanest city award in the first *Swachh Survekshan* in 2016.

Since then, Indore city has undertaken a huge cleanliness drive; its examples are given worldwide. A plan was also chalked out systematically to motivate the people of Indore towards cleanliness.

Plan Formation

Indore was ranked 180 in 2015 in terms of cleanliness. In 2016, when the *Swachh Survekshan* was conducted for the first time in the country, Indore lagged behind most cities. The city received the 25th ranking. When Prime

Minister Narendra Modi conveyed the concept of *Swachh Survekshan* to the country, the corporation and the district administration, together with the local people and public representatives, started an exercise to prepare a new cleanliness module. Till the Corporation elections in 2014, a private company A2Z was responsible for cleaning the city. Despite numerous efforts, the company failed to keep the city clean.

Resource Challenges

The new council of the corporation decided to first take up the cleanliness issue. Then the question also arose: the corporation does not have many resources and enough people; how will cleanliness happen? For this, the Mayor and the Corporation first began to lay emphasis on their resources. They were regularly on the lookout for more resources. After making a complete list of resources, a list of employees in the corporation was also made. Once the list was made, it was understood that many of them had not reported for duty at all. They were irresponsible in doing their jobs. Only the formal supply was being done.

The zonal offices were in the worst condition. Strict actions were decided to be taken. More than 700 regular and temporary workers were either suspended or fired. This strict action sent out a message among the employees that their job will be saved only if they worked. The corporation then called up all the employees to get into action. Everyone began to feel that they will soon be out of jobs if the work was not done. However, since its inception till now, the sanitation workers of the corporation have been completing their work with full devotion. There is a desire in them to keep their city clean and to attain the number one position in the country again and again. By imposing strictness, the whole scenario changed.

Scrap Vehicles did the work

Often, the habit of crying for insufficient resources is common. Many items are said to be out of fashion, thus giving rise to lots of junk. Indore also had this traditional habit. Many useful vehicles of the Municipal Corporation were thrown as junk after a minor malfunction. When Indore involved itself in the cleanliness drive, the first big question was how to arrange the vehicles to collect door-to-door wastage. As the question itself, the problem was also big, but by following 'Where there is a will, there is a way', the corporation picked out and checked the vehicles parked in the garage as junk. The vehicles that needed minor repairing were repaired.

The corporation got 200 vehicles from this scrap for use. With just 200 vehicles, it undertook the cleanliness drive, which slowly gained acceleration. In just two years of the cleanliness drive, the corporation increased the vehicle count to 700. Of these, around 400 small vehicles are only for garbage collection. Presently, there is no shortage of any kind of resource in collecting garbage.

First Survey

To make the city clean, the corporation formulated a plan to prevent open defecation. Instead of torturing, criticising or rebuking the open defecators, the corporation's administration worked on to change their mindset. For this, a survey was conducted to find the most common places where people go for open defecation. After studying the report, toilets were built rapidly in those areas.

End of Open Defecation

For ensuring the success of the *Swachh Bharat* Mission, other works were also stopped in the city wards for three months. They had only one goal, which was to complete the work of the *Swachh Bharat* Mission fast before the deadline. The corporation built accessible toilets in busy and congested areas of the city; made toilets and corporation vehicles accessible to slum dwellers. The impact of the corporation's efforts was such that people changed their mindset about open defecation. Strict prohibition was also applied at some places.

Success Achieved

The year 2017 proved to be a breakthrough for the city of Indore. Indore city achieved the number one position in cleanliness drive among 434 cities, considering it to be the cleanest city in the country. This gave a boost to the Municipal Corporation and it increased the work.

Removal of Trash Boxes

After that, a campaign was launched for cleanliness throughout the city. The corporation took a strong decision to remove garbage boxes from the city since most of the garbage materials were dumped on the street road in the city; people and shopkeepers dumped garbage around the garbage boxes. In order to get rid of this, garbage was collected from house to house and from shops to shops. If garbage collection was successful in some areas, boxes were removed from those areas first. Later, garbage boxes were removed from the entire city. This decision was most appreciated. At the same time, wet and dry wastage was collected separately from the houses in the city. Municipal vehicles started going to people's homes to collect garbage twice a day. Not only this, but corporation employees were also put on duty in three shifts to clean the city.

The theme song designed for the cleanliness of Indore has its own role in this case. The memory of the first theme song recorded in the voice of singer Shaan still reverberates in the hearts of the people. On hearing this, it became a routine for people to remove garbage from their homes and dump it into the vehicles. Now it has become a never-ending habit.

Mass Campaign Launched

The need for a new system for the disposal of wastage was clearly visible. The old cleaning agency was replaced.

The infrastructure was built, and the municipal workshop was given a new lease of life and makeover since it would not have been possible to lift the garbage of such a big city with the initial model. A huge public awareness campaign was started in the city, in which dignitaries along with political leaders were involved.

Trenching Ground Creation

Trenching grounds were built to collect garbage from across the city. Polythene was first isolated from the wastes brought in. Composting was done from the leftover waste materials. While the pages were used for road construction, paper blocks were also made. These blocks are situated in many places in the city.

Spot Fine

Indore was the first city in the country to impose a fine for spitting on the road. For this, corporation vehicles are constantly patrolling. *Paan* cart dealers across the city were given strict instructions that if any garbage, *paan* peaks or wrappers were seen outside their shops, penalty would be strictly imposed. The imposition of a fine was implemented throughout the city. Fine was imposed amounting to millions of rupees. Finally, the people realised their responsibilities. They stopped spitting or littering. As a result, Indore has remained number one in cleanliness since the year 2017.

Once a tourist vehicle from Kerala crossed Rajwada in Indore. A tourist threw the wrapper of a biscuit on the road from the vehicle. After that, the corporation's car followed them for 2 km., intercepted them and imposed a fine for that action. People aboard the vehicle were stunned by this incident, although they also praised the public's passion for cleanliness in Indore.

Team Work

When Indore was first selected as the cleanest city in the country, it was a collective effort by a team. The team members were Mayor Malini Gaur, Collector P. Narhari, and Manish Singh. The Mayor changed the way the Indore Municipal Corporation functioned. Collector P. Narhari took strict administrative action where necessary. Manish Singh worked vigorously that the entire image of the Municipal Corporation was changed. In addition to all this, the people of the city left no stone unturned in making Indore clean. It was busy implementing every rule of the corporation.

Increased Earnings from the Waste Management

Along with cleanliness, they were attentive about waste management. They gained financial benefits from it. In the financial year 2019-20, the urban body's earnings from wet and dry waste processing increased by 50 percent to nearly 6 crore rupees. In the financial year 2018-19, IMC generated about 4 crore rupees from waste processing.

Waste Disposal

For dry waste, the Municipal Corporation set up an automated processing plant with Artificial Intelligence. Through this plant, glass, plastic, paper, cardboard, metal, etc., are removed separately from the dry waste. The corporation is making CNG gas and compost manure by processing the wet waste. For the processing of wet waste, the corporation is setting up a new bio-CNG plant of 500 tonnes capacity in the Devguradia area of the city based on Public-Private Partnership (PPP).

A private company will invest around Rs. 250 crores in the new plant, while the corporation will provide space for this unit and wet waste for processing.

Mountain of Garbage Removed

The corporation also removed the mountain of garbage collected over the years on the trenching ground with this waste management. Earlier, it was also difficult to even pass from there due to the stench; now, people have tea and snacks in the garden laid out there.

Buses Run on CNG

The corporation found that most of the wet waste originated from the vegetable market. For this, a bio-CNG plant was built there. The city buses run on gas produced in the plant. The corporation is also generating revenue from this. This model of cleanliness has spread the fame of Indore not only in the country but also abroad. Many delegations from abroad have come to understand the cleanliness model of Indore. The Municipal Corporation has also started charging fees for this. The corporation has started earning from this as well.

The Plan

In the financial year, 2021-22, the Municipal Corporation's earnings from processing wet and dry waste in individual plants have increased to around Rs. 10 crores. According to the corporation's officials, in a city with a population of about 3.5 million, the corporation has developed the ability to safely dispose about 1,200 tons of garbage every day in different ways. This includes 550 tons of wet waste and 650 tons of dry waste.

Public Support

The city's people played an important role in making Indore number one in the cleanliness for the fifth time. Nearly 3 lakh people of Indore have given positive feedback in *'Swachh Survekshan'*. This also helped the city in getting a bonus in the title of cleanliness. Nearly 4 lakh people downloaded the Indore-311 app to clean and solve the municipal corporation's problems in the city. Out of this, more than 3,05,000 people gave feedback in *'Swachh Survekshan'* through the app and other means. With this, the city started trying to put a premium on cleanliness. The city has now also started efforts to become a Seven Star City.

An old popular phrase is *'Aam Ke Aam, Guthli Ke Daam'*. The people of Indore make this phrase come true every day. Indore is a commercial city and here, everything from a needle to an elephant is well-utilised. A few years ago, waste was a problem in Indore. Today, waste has become a source of income. Making organic manure from wet waste has become a regular source of income for the people. Making diesel and CNG from dry waste has paved a new way for creating various possibilities from waste. Interlocking tiles are also being constructed from waste building material.

The most different and most unique work one will get

to see is on the trenching ground. There was a time when the main objective of the cleanliness campaign in the city was to collect garbage from people's homes.

The work of collecting garbage also started, and the garbage coming out of the houses started getting collected in the trenching ground. The collected garbage very soon turned into a mountain. Approximately 700 tonnes of garbage were collected daily from the entire city. If there is a problem, there is also a solution.

The Municipal Corporation also made arrangements to tackle this problem. After the waste was levelled in the same ground, small fruit plants were planted all around the trenching ground. In a way, fencing of the field was done with these plants. The environment began to be beautiful and safe. Along with the Indore Municipal Corporation and District Administration, the speciality of Indore is that they do not undertake the work just for the sake of doing it, but do the work with utmost responsibility.

In this sequence, the plants planted in the trenching ground started getting regular care. Small fruit plants have grown tall and are swaying like trees. The fruits on these trees attract people towards them. Trenching ground in-charge Bharat Singh Chauhan says that most plants planted in the trenching ground have become trees.

Many of these have started giving fruits, and the remaining trees will also bear fruits in the near future. According to the trenching ground in-charge, 7 jackfruit plants, 47 mango plants, 15 guava plants, 50 banana plants, 35 *sitaphal* plants and 28 plants of *chiku* were planted in the ground.

There is a plan to sell the fruits borne of these trees. Upon obtaining the decision of the Municipal Corporation, its sale to the general public will be commenced. It is important to learn from Indore how they succeeded in converting a mountain of garbage into blooming green trees and plants. How to make the city beautiful in Indore with planned efforts was learnt and taken forward with cleanliness. We should appreciate and keep our environment clean.

□

4

Indore and ODF

The Indore Municipal Corporation was declared as Open Defecation Free (ODF) city in 2017 by the Quality Council of India, authorised institute of the Government of India.

In 2018, Indore was the first city to be declared as ODF++ in the country by the Government of India for achieving sanitation sustainability. In order to make Indore city ODF and achieve this goal, more than 12,713 single toilets were made during the survey in all 85 wards of Indore city. Regular updates were made on the Government of India's portal. Similarly, the Indore Municipal Corporation has constructed 120 community toilets and 209 public toilets in commercial areas and other important areas. To ensure tap connection in every single toilet, CT/PT, about 15 crores was spent installing 122 tube-wells, 94 km pipelines, and 689 water tanks. All these measures were taken to make the city of Indore ODF, which was also recognised by the Government of India and it was considered an important achievement of Indore.

All the community and public toilets have full facilities as per the Government of India's ODF+ guidelines. They have been made suitable for their use by differently-abled persons (*Divyangjan*) and children, and separate arrangements were made for use by women so that no one faces any inconvenience or problem. Flowing water, proper light, ramps as well as ventilation were provided in the toilets for convenience.

Sanitary napkin vending machines have been installed in the toilets for hygiene of women. A feedback machine has also been installed for the public in the toilets to get the users' feedback in real time. Anyone can register their complaint about the non-availability of cleanliness facilities or support. An online mechanism is also in place to take action against the issues raised by the user. Sanitation facilities of the toilets are revamped based on the feedback received from the users of the toilets. All these toilets have also been geotagged on Google toilet locator for public convenience.

The facility of public toilets for women and men is also provided at petrol pumps situated within the city of Indore. Arrangements have also been made at these places as per the instructions of the Government of India. Maintenance and quality of toilets are done through the city's industrial establishments and from the revenue of the outdoor advertising agency. For the sanitation of the city of Indore, it is necessary to ensure regular cleaning of the septic tanks. For this, an agency was entrusted with removing silt from all the septic tanks in the city by assigning work based on priority and experience. If an obstacle in the silt disposal was observed, then the agency was also entrusted with the responsibility of transporting the silt extracted from the septic tank to the treatment plant, where the silt is disposed of. Silt disposal is done at the sewage treatment plant at Kabir Khedi.

Sewer Treatment Plants (STP) with a capacity of 12 MLD, 78 MLD and 245 MLD are situated at Kabir Khedi. The sewage originating from the city of Indore is processed from these plants, and the clean water is tested as per the prescribed standards and re-cleaned and released back. In order to keep the city of Indore at the forefront of the *Swachh Bharat* Mission, the work of garbage collection and execution is being done in a well-planned manner.

By making timely treatment of sewage and making the water usable, the city's water problem is being resolved, and the city has become free from dirt and diseases. Sanitation has been included in the lifestyle of Indore, and it is an ongoing process. Sanitation and Indore are connected strongly to each other. Indore is proving to be a role model for the whole country in the matter of sanitation. And the combined efforts of the administration, Municipal Corporation, sanitation workers and the people of Indore are proving fruitful.

□

5

Yes, We Can

Women Played a Pivotal Role in Making Indore the Cleanest City

Anita Sharma, a responsible homemaker, is a resident of Badri Bagh Colony in Indore. She admits, "Earlier, before the 'Clean City' drive, it was easier to toss every waste item into just one bucket and dump it the next day in the municipal trash bin. But when the *Swachh Bharat Abhiyan* was launched, the first move by the administration was the removal of these municipal garbage bins from every locality".

"We were shocked!" she confesses. What next was an unanswerable and disturbing question that kept popping into our heads and in the neighbourhood chats for a couple of days. I used to express my discontent with my next-door friends who were equally baffled by the municipality's decision."

"Then we came across the 'new' cleanliness concept and the awareness programme being propagated by our able administrative officers and personnel through FM radio channels, local television and door-to-door word of mouth affirmations that the administration is going to collect 'wet' and 'dry' wastes separately from every doorstep and henceforth manage it efficiently."

They urged the people of Indore to have two bins in their homes and explained the concept of 'wet waste' and 'dry waste', said Anita.

"How will this be possible?" asked my surprised mother-in-law. "Why are they doing this?" and many other such related questions originated from everyone's minds.

Soon, a municipal collection van started door-to-door collection of waste from dawn up to late evening. It played a very peppy and melodious song sung by singer Shaan. This song quickly conquered our hearts, and it became the second hymn after our morning prayer. Its lyrics were very captivating and motivated us to play our part as responsible Indoris and discard every waste item into proper 'dry' or 'wet' bin.

"It was not as difficult as we were assuming it to be!" chuckles Mrs. Sharma. In fact, it just takes a second to think what type of waste it is and in which bin it should be disposed".

"It has now become our daily routine to throw the trash into its appropriate bins. Every member of my family does it easily."

On the other hand, Mr. and Mrs. Shah have a different tale to tell. They reveal that they found the concept of 'dry and wet' categorisation difficult initially and could not do it as they were both busy working individuals and often ran out of time for this little extra effort. Both of them couldn't segregate the waste and even got into a rift with the garbage collector who refused to segregate their waste manually after a few days.

"We were annoyed and irritated but noticed that everyone in our vicinity had adopted this new practice with ease. We even repeatedly overheard conversations at our respective workplaces regarding the benefits of this new concept".

"My colleagues, mostly women, shared their successful experiences of 'dry and wet' categorisation with me. This began to inspire us. I think the seeds of change were sown in our hearts!" smiles Mrs. Shah.

"The local news revealed how efficiently the administration was converting the entire city's wet waste into manure and helping the farmers. We realised the virtue of this cause. Our ancestors were also from agricultural backgrounds. So, we too, decided to be a farmer's friend. Just a little effort was all that was needed from us, and we would definitely do it", a very optimistic Mr. Shah recalls his wife's words.

"By now, my wife was convinced with this favourable change and was all set to take it on", he declared merrily.

"My wife and I embraced this new idea and marched our way forward along with our locality neighbours towards a cleaner and greener Indore."

These two and many more similar instances prove that the women of Indore had a very important role in making the *Swachh Bharat Abhiyan* such a huge success. The unmatched efforts of the administration and the ongoing awareness programmes created to help the people realise the importance of separately categorising 'wet and dry wastes' helped make the waste collection a profitable proposition.

The local administration launched an aggressive campaign to motivate the people towards this new beneficial change via electronic media like radio, television, and internet and print media like local newspapers and weekly magazines. The playing of a lively and encouraging song in the garbage collection van was a sure move to make people feel energetic and high spirited towards the successful achievement of this mission.

The administration received unprecedented support from the women of Indore. These brave responsible women not only changed themselves, but they prompted every member of their family to adopt the latest cleanliness practice. When the homemaker decides to take a clean call, all family members dutifully abide by it. Household waste constitutes a large part of any city's waste. Its methodical segregation and collection at the very basic level from individual homes were made possible by the incredible contribution of women.

The consumption of plastic in the city also reduced manifolds due to the efforts of smart women of Indore who adopted the "Carry Your Own Bag" (CYOB) concept when they stepped out for grocery shopping. In addition to this, these intelligent women prioritised carrying their own bottle of water while going out. Thus, the city witnessed an appreciable reduction in plastic waste.

The involvement of women in this cleanliness drive is unparalleled. They wholeheartedly accepted the practice of correctly segregating the wet and dry waste items right from the start of the day. They accurately disposed of the wet organic kitchen wastes like eggshells, tea leaves, vegetable and fruit peels and minimalistic food wastes into the 'wet' bin. On the other hand, dry rubbish, papers, broken stuff, plastic and other scraps are collected in separate 'dry' bins. This has become a custom of every household in Indore.

This incident dates back to 2015. Indore, which is recognised as the commercial capital of Madhya Pradesh, was also no different from other cities of the country. Stray cattle and other animals could be seen roaming in the lanes, streets, near traffic squares and near garbage thrown recklessly on the roadsides. Things used to get worse in the rainy season. Not surprisingly, Indore was ranked 180th in the cleanliness survey conducted by the Government of India in 2015. But this year was very important for Indore. In 2015, Indore set out on a journey that would give it a different identity nationally and globally.

On the occasion of Gandhi Jayanti on 2nd October 2015, Prime Minister Narendra Modi urged people to fulfil Mahatma Gandhi's dream for a clean and hygienic India and regard cleanliness as a campaign. It is difficult to say how the rest of the country responded to this appeal, but during this time, the command of Indore Municipal Corporation was in the hands of a woman. In the same year, Mrs. Malini Gaur took charge as Mayor of Indore Municipal Corporation. She decided to change the appearance of Indore and make it a clean and litter-free city.

The result was that a year later, in the Swachhta *Survekshan* of 2016, Indore jumped from the 180th position to the 25th position in a single big leap. But Indore was yet to carve a niche for itself as the cleanest city and get appreciated nationally and globally. It took another year to achieve this dream. Now this medium-sized city of Madhya Pradesh has been recognised and hailed in the whole country. In the year 2017, Indore had become the leader in cleanliness after beating 434 cities of the country. Since then, Indore has topped five times in a row in the cleanliness surveys of the Government of India. Now the people of the city are gearing up to be number one for the sixth successive time and put a 'cleanliness Chakka' in the cleanliness survey 2022.

Many factors contributed to this great success of Indore. Undoubtedly, Indore's cleanliness drive could accomplish this feat because of the unrelenting support and cooperation received from every section of society. But it would be no exaggeration to say that the role or participation of women was most vital as the women power made Indore the cleanest city for five times successively.

By the way, the relationship between cleanliness and women in Indian society is quite deep and significant. In most families, women shoulder the responsibility of keeping the home clean. It is evident that the role of women in the cleanliness of the city has also been very important. In the cleanliness surveys, the role of women in making Indore number one can be categorised in the following manner:

- Women leadership
- Role of women sanitation workers
- Role of homemakers and working women

Women Leadership

As the Mayor of the Indore Municipal Corporation, Mrs. Malini Gaur took the first bold step to make Indore clean. This step was to remove thousands of big garbage bins kept in the entire city because the trash was usually found around these garbage bins. The things had come to such a state that people hesitated to go close to bins and dump garbage into them as there was so much dirt and filth around the bins and a foul smell always emanated from the rotting garbage. As a result, the garbage was also thrown outside these bins, which used to decay and spread all over when the wind blew.

But the question was if the bins were removed, where the waste generated in the houses would go. With the help of her able officers, the mayor worked on putting in place a system for collecting garbage from 4 lakh houses in the city. Garbage collection vehicles were repaired. Instead of appealing to the people to dump garbage in the right place, the Municipal Corporation started collecting garbage from the people's homes.

Role of Women Workers

It is evident that many employees were also needed for this campaign of the Municipal Corporation to collect garbage from house to house. At that time, there was a ban on new recruitments at the government level, but they managed to find a way, and recruited daily wage workers. Mayor Malini Gaur understood very well that more and more women would have to be associated with this campaign to set an example in cleanliness. In such a situation, more opportunities were provided to them, and preference was given to women during the recruitment of sanitation staff.

The importance of this work was explained to the new women workers. They were told how important their role was in making Indore clean and enhancing its prestige. These women also realised that their work was not small or insignificant but very important in pushing the cleanliness drive towards the finish line.

□

6

True Testimonials from Real Life Warriors

Madhya Pradesh's largest city Indore remains at the top of the country in terms of cleanliness. The credit for this success goes to the local people and the sanitation workers who believe that cleanliness is their *karma* and *dharma*. When Indore wore the crown of cleanliness for the first time, it became clear that it was made possible only due to the people's awareness through which this success was achieved.

Those late-night workers engaged in cleaning the entire city along with the common people have shown Indore to the world as the cleanest city. Usually, the public's opinion about municipal employees-officers is that they do not effectively discharge their responsibilities, but this is not the case in Indore. Here, the officers and employees of the Municipal Corporation do not wait for orders; rather, they dutifully do their work. As the night progresses, when people retire for the day, the city sanitation workers and the Municipal Corporation's vehicles are busy keeping the city clean. They can be seen completing their work with full vigour irrespective of the season.

There are 85 wards in the city of Indore, which the Municipal Corporation has divided into 15 zones after a careful study. It is estimated that six wards fall under one zone of the Municipal Corporation. The entire community of the Municipal Corporation is so hardworking that there is hardly any complaint from any ward regarding negligence or the quality of their work. Rather, it is for the residents to change their old habits. The sanitation workers of the corporation are so strict that they do not listen to any influential persons. Instead, they advise them with humility. If they don't listen, then they do not hesitate to take action. Everyone came forward towards this drive for cleanliness and started keeping dustbins in their homes. However, there were certain obstacles down the way. The corporation employees struggled hard to get rid of the habit of putting wet and dry garbage together.

Many influential people used their influence to bully the sanitation workers of the corporation, but it did not affect them. The sanitation workers were ordered by the corporation commissioner, mayor and collector not to compromise on cleanliness. Waste segregation into wet and dry has now become a habit among the public. In case of any error, the sanitation workers talk it out and go through the process again. The good thing is that after the hard work of the Municipal Corporation, it became possible to help the public understand the concept of waste segregation.

Renu Bai, who has been working as a sanitation worker in the Municipal Corporation since 1989, says that they were enjoying their work in these years. Earlier, they worked for their survival, but now they were very happy that Indore is the most beautiful and clean city. Now she along with her fellow workers does not worry about the working hours. The concern now is that no assigned locality should remain dirty. Praising her officers, she says that now the officers are all educated, including her supervisor who understands their problem. He also praises their work and helps them. If there is any complaint about bullying by the public, immediate action is taken. They have resolved to keep the city clean not only for today but forever.

Along with Renu Bai, Radha Shankar, who is also a sanitation worker, has a glow on her face about Indore. She says that when people praise Indore for cleanliness, it seems that they are praising us. We are doing our jobs, but due to the support and cooperation of the people of Indore, we can do our work properly. She is very happy with the behaviour of the officers. She says that it is now difficult to know who an officer is and who is an employee. Together we keep our Indore clean. Sir, when people from outside praise our Indore, we feel happy. The praise is worth more than money. It would be nice if our Indore remains clean like this forever.

Another sanitation worker, Chhote Lal, says that their duty starts late at night. They work in three different shifts. Earlier, they only used to work when it pleased them, but they have changed their habits. If someone falls ill or does not come to work for any reason, then they come forward and do his work. In a way, they have also become responsible to each other. They all aim to make Indore cleaner. They are glad that everyone appreciates their work.

Rajesh, a cleaning worker also agrees with his colleagues. He says that the city is ours. If this city is giving us bread and clothes to eat, then the responsibility of elevating its name is also ours. Today, the triumph of Indore is now visible all over the country; all Indoris together have made this city clean. We will continue to strive in the future to ensure that our Indore always remains number one.

Himanshu Gupta is a sanitary inspector. According to him, hygiene among people was a far cry earlier, but now people have adopted it in their lifestyle.

The best thing is that they do not allow the city to get dirty, and if someone accidentally threw any garbage, then the chorus of people shouting– "brother, put it in the garbage bin" can be heard. Sanitary Inspector Gupta says that on-the-spot fines were imposed to prevent people from littering garbage. The fine imposed was so hefty that it prevented the person from littering again. Polythene and thermocol products have been completely banned, leading to a reduction in plastic usage. Bag Bank (*Thaila* Bank) and Utensil Bank (*Bartan* Bank), a new habit which is prevalent among the people too is proving helpful in keeping the city clean.

The Indore Municipal Corporation (IMC) has always valued its *Safai Mitras*, and from time to time, through various measures, it attempts to motivate and encourage the *safai mitras* who work day and night, regardless of the weather conditions to keep the city clean and green.

Consequently, the IMC recognises the hard work and efforts made by the *safai mitras* by appreciating and celebrating them. For instance, every month, it identifies the *safai mitras* who have worked particularly hard during the current month and awards them.

Simultaneously, it also conducted a ward level awareness drive called *Swachhta* Inspection, wherein it introduced the ward residents to the *safai mitras* deployed in the ward. This bridged the gap between the workers and the *safai mitras* and the residents and paved the way for better communication and interaction between them. The residents felicitated the *safai mitras* with garlands and applause.

Till a few years ago, the Municipal Corporation staff would have been doing only those jobs allocated to them, but now they have become responsible towards their city and are aware of their duty. The ban on single use plastic in the country was also started from Indore.

In the city, the use of straws, suspension plates, spoons etc., has considerably reduced. On major roads, cleaning is done at night with 23 machines. The garbage is collected and dumped first thing in the morning. Many places in the city do not produce waste, as they convert that into compost. 45,000 houses in the city are equipped with home composting units.

Because of these steps, there is a significant decrease in waste material. Hefty fines are imposed for throwing garbage and spitting on the streets. The Municipal Corporation generates revenue of Rs. 30 lakhs each year from these fines.

The caregivers themselves undertake the cleaning duties and are so engrossed in their work that they don't even bother to take a vacation.

Along with the cleaning staff, the corporation commissioner, additional commissioner, zonal officers and other top officers go to the site early in the morning to monitor the cleaning work.

The corporation has more than 1,150 vehicles for collecting garbage. Indore has 425 urinals and 225 community toilets, which are regularly cleaned. Due to the above facilities available in all major areas, people do not defecate in the open. There is an app developed by the residents of Indore to identify these toilets. This has been integrated with the 311 app of the IMC.

The effectiveness of the cleanliness drive has made everyone own Indore. It is an ongoing drive, which people live daily. In this sense, they own and make this different from other cities. Whether you call it the culture of Indore or lifestyle or say "Wow, Indore, Wow", Indore is also included in the selected cities of the country, where the residents dispose of the wet and dry waste discharged from their homes within their premises. It is also the first city in the country where residents get money from waste, which is a big incentive. Indore is the only city where the bank formula has been adopted for the sake of cleanliness.

In order to reduce the amount of waste, two cloth bags or *Jhola* bag bank, four pot or *Bartan* banks, a 'wall of righteousness' for old clothes, and food ATMs are working to bring ready and leftover food to the needy.

The Food Bank's plan has proved to be very effective in reducing the amount of wet waste. There are different schemes of waste management in processing the foundation of success in the sanitation of Indore. This includes 550 tonnes of wet waste and 650 tonnes of dry waste and about 8,500 cleaners' work in three shifts continuously from 6 am to 4 am, keeping the city clean.

The corporation also earns Rs. 80 lakh from advertising in the urinal and toilet stands. Free steel utensils are made available in various programmes through the *bartan* bank to reduce the use of disposable plates.

Apart from this, bags of cloth are provided to the people through *Jhola* Bank as an alternative. The common people of Indore have now become so responsible that if someone accidentally throws anything on the road, others will either pick it up and dispose of it themselves or politely ask that person to do so. Although this cleanliness campaign was launched on Prime Minister Narendra Modi's call, the credit goes to the local people and sanitation workers.

Now let us know why Indore got the Award.

Indore is the first city in India where 100 % waste

processing of building material and waste collection and construction material disposal is being done.

Indore is the first city where new experiments have been started, thereby completely eliminating the trenching ground.

Arrangements of GPS Control Rooms and Zones to look after garbage vehicles in Indore have been made.

It is the first city in the country where 100% of the people dispose of the garbage out of their houses to their right place.

Home composting work is being done with wet waste in more than nine thousand houses in Indore

Indore is the first city where two Zero Waste events were organised in the presence of millions of people.

The foundation of success in the cleanliness of Indore has different schemes of waste management and processing.

The city has developed a capacity to dispose of about 1,200 tonnes of waste every day safely.

This includes 550 tonnes of wet waste and 650 tonnes of dry waste.

Around 8,500 sweepers work in three shifts continuously from 6 am to 4am in the city to keep it clean.

Large garbage boxes have been removed from the city long back.

Wet and dry waste from every house and commercial establishment is collected separately by 700 vehicles of the IMC.

Bio-wastes like used diapers and sanitary napkins are separately kept in garbage collection vehicles so that they can be easily disposed of.

Waste processing plants in the city are set up on the basis of Public-Private Partnership (PPP) in order to be financially sustainable.

Nearly 35,000 houses in Indore have manure units made from wet wastes.

Wet waste coming out of houses is reduced due to the waste making units.

With the establishment of '*Thaila* Bank' and '*Bartan* Bank,' the IMC has made the homes, hotels and restaurants plastic-free. Innovative steps like 'FOOD ATM' have also been taken to make food available to the needy.

The use of single-use plastic products has already been banned in Indore.

About 12% of sewage treated water is reused in the IMC's 25 orchards.

□

7

Sanitation Helped Curb Diseases

Sanitation and disease are closely linked to each other. If you live in a clean environment, you remain safe from diseases and germs, but if your surroundings are not clean and fresh, then before long, diseases and disease-causing germs will get you.

The relationship between sanitation and disease was clearly visible during the conceptualisation and realisation of Clean Indore.

There was a time when there used to be crowds of patients in hospitals, clinics and medical stores, but the situation has changed in the last few years.

Indore's brilliant success has brought glory to the country and motivated people to give up their unhealthy lifestyles and lead a healthy life, leading to less sickness. Fewer people now visit the hospitals, and fewer customers are seen at medical stores. Doctors and medical shops consider it a good sign for Indore's better life. They say that along with the older people, youngsters too were falling victim to many diseases. It was frightening to see Indore slowly turning into a city of diseases, but the administration and residents associated with the *Swachh Bharat Abhiyan* saved the city from sickness and unhealthy routine. Sanitation has a direct impact on health and reduces airborne diseases. No one thought that sanitation would yield such a positive result. But surveys have confirmed this fact.

Ayushman, 25, was stressed and upset for a long time. He felt that he was in the grip of some major disease. Upon doctors' advice, he started going on morning walks and gave up unhealthy eating habits, but even after that, he was not getting better. But since the last few months, he has been feeling fresh and fine and follows a regular and natural routine. When analysed what could be the reason behind the change, he realised that earlier he had to cover his nose and mouth at most places in Indore. It was difficult to walk due to the dirt and foul smell. But as Indore became cleaner, the stench and dirt disappeared, and his inner tension began to dissipate. However, even today, Ayushman covers his face and nose as a precautionary measure.

Along with Ayushman, Sumi Jain, studying management at a local college, suffered from persistent cough. Doctors conducted several check-ups and gave different treatments, but they couldn't find the exact reason behind her ailment. No one in her family had asthma or respiratory disease, thus ruling out any hereditary disease. Like Ayushman, Sumi too feels that she is getting relief from her persistent cough. When she examined her routine, she found that it was the same as before, but she had gotten better without any medical treatment. Sumi is thankful to *Swachh Bharat*

Abhiyan and the cleanliness in Indore.

Indore, which has become the leader in the *Swachhta Survekshan* in the country, is also moving towards better health by climbing the ladder of cleanliness. The results of the ongoing sanitation mission in Indore are now coming to the fore. The direct effect of removing garbage bins from the city, door-to-door collection of domestic waste and curbing open defecation is visible in the city's health and atmosphere. In order to monitor the ground realities, the Indore Municipal Corporation recently conducted a survey in which doctors, members of the Drug Association and the Indian Medical Association were also involved. The Municipal Corporation and Health Department claim that there is an estimated 70% reduction in diseases spread by pollution, as per the survey's findings.

The decline in the sale of medicines by Rs. 30 crores proves that the spread of diseases has been largely curbed. According to the health department, earlier, more than one lakh patients with diseases like jaundice, cholera, vomiting, diarrhoea, hepatitis, malaria and dengue etc., used to visit the hospitals before the Covid-19 spread. About 1,000 patients used to be treated daily in OPD. But in the quarter from June to August 2021, only about 35,000 patients visited hospitals daily. These included patients suffering from other diseases as well.

Rameshwar Bhai, who runs a grocery shop in Rajwada, says that he had respiratory problems due to dust and dirt; he could not get relief even after taking medicines as advised by the doctors. The doctors told him to avoid dust and dirt, but while living in Rajwada, it was difficult to do so. He is now happy that dust and dirt have almost disappeared due to the clean Indore campaign, and now he is now rid of his breathing problem. He is thankful to the administration for this and tries to keep the city and his house clean. Along with Rameshwar Bhai, his 55-year-old wife Vishnupriya is also enjoying better health. She and all other members of her family are pure vegetarians. But Vishnupriya always suffered from fatigue and tiredness. Her face had a weathering look, but then the sanitation campaign started in Indore, and the city became clean. She no longer feels tired and stays fit and fine. The couple's activities may have been reduced due to age, but they don't have to visit hospitals and doctors.

A young couple Rekha and Ramesh, both around 30, was worried about their small child. The doctors conducted many tests and prescribed different treatments as 5-year-old Priyank was not active as other children.

Rekha and Ramesh were anxious for their child. But they

soon began to notice some changes in Priyank. He started waking up on time and began playing. When they consulted the doctor about this, the doctor was also surprised. When he inquired about further treatment, Rekha and Ramesh said it was not needed.

While engaged in conversation with the doctor, they noticed a pile of garbage in the area where they lived. Everyone used to throw garbage near their house. After regular cleaning began being conducted, the cause of the sickness was revealed. The doctor explained to Ramesh and Rekha that due to pollution, Priyank had become lethargic. As he was now living in a cleaner environment, he was becoming as active as other kids of his age.

Many such cases prove that *Swachh* Indore has brought laurels to the city and has also provided fresh air and a pollution-free environment to the people. Madhusudan Mandloi, the civil surgeon of the district hospital, said that people in Indore have become healthier due to proper sanitation.

There has been a 15% decrease in medicines given free to people from the hospitals. At the same time, no person died due to dengue in Indore before the Covid-19 pandemic spread. The quality of air has improved due to sanitation. Due to this change, immunity of the people is also increasing day by day. That is why they are able to fight diseases. Dr. Sanjay Londe, president of the Indore Medical Association, said that Indore has achieved the goal of better health. Earlier, during summer and monsoon, crowds of patients could be seen at doctors' clinics. But now the diseases have decreased by 10 to 70 %. The sale of glucose and electrol powder came down by about Rs. 20 crores in the year 2020.

Vinay Bakliwal, president of the Indore Chemist Association, said that sales of medicines for the treatment of liver diseases and dehydration have decreased by about 70%. Between the months of May and August in the year 2021, about Rs. 20 crores worth of glucose, electrol powder, etc., could not be sold in the Indore drug market. Earlier, medicines worth Rs. 8-10 crores used to be sold in a 3–4-month period to treat common fever, dysentery, diarrhoea, besides analgesic drugs, antibiotics etc. But now, the sale of these medicines has dipped substantially. The sale of medicines for urine infections has also decreased by 60%.

Reduction in the following Diseases

Diseases caused by contaminated water, diarrhoea, jaundice and common fever.

Diseases caused by mosquitoes, houseflies etc., like malaria, dengue, chikungunya, cholera and other bacterial diseases.

Percentage Reduction in Diseases

Diarrhoea	-	60%
Jaundice	-	70%
Malaria	-	up to 30%
Cholera	-	40%
Dengue	-	10 to 15%

Survey Conducted by the Municipal Corporation

According to administration sources, the results of the tough decisions taken in the city are now coming to the fore. The immunity of people is much better. Due to sanitation, residents' health is better than before, and this is a big achievement. Dr Uttam Yadav, the health officer of the corporation, says that all the doctors, drug associations, drug dealers and hospitals were surveyed, and it was found that the sale of medicines had dipped and the number of people falling ill had come down substantially.

Reduction in Pollution

The level of pollution is continuously increasing throughout the country. But the atmosphere in the cleanest city of the country, Indore, has improved rapidly. Indore has worked with determination for the proper disposal of waste.

A monthly report of 51 districts of the state is released every month by the Pollution Control Board. In this, the most polluted district is ranked first. Indore has always occupied the 35th place in this list, although it is the industrial capital of the state. Officials of other cities of the country too come here to see the efforts made in the city regarding the environment.

Removal of Dust

The Municipal Corporation had started cleaning the city's streets to help Indore reach the number one place in sanitation. The major roads of the city are cleaned by machines every night. This wiped out the city's dust. Diseases caused by dust have also been controlled to a great extent. The municipal corporation first started collecting the waste from houses. They removed the garbage bins where people used to throw domestic trash. This cleared all the dirt from the city. This had a direct impact on health. The biggest problem of the city was the trenching ground at Devguradia. People living within a radius of 5 km of the trenching ground always complained of cough and other respiratory problems. Earlier, plastic bags were popular in the city. IMC staff and the people used to burn them in open places. This spread poisonous smoke and made people ill, but now with the ban on plastics, people can breathe easier.

Cleaning of River Kahn

The drains which polluted the Kahn River were diverted. The polluted water emanating from the Sanwer Road Industrial Area industries was stopped from flowing into the river. Plantations were planted on the banks of the river. All this directly impacted the health of the people living in the slums around the river. The Municipal Corporation set up a plant in Kabit Khedi for the treatment of contaminated water.

Treatment of sewage water was carried out here. It was used for construction works in the city and to irrigate the plants. It has also helped in preventing diseases. The Municipal Corporation is now focusing on reducing waste in the colonies. The wet waste will be disposed of in the colonies.

Srigopal Jagtap, supporting the corporation's waste management project, says that some families have started making manure from wet waste at home. The focus will be on preparing manure from wet waste at homes to be used by people for irrigating plants and trees growing in their homes and nearby places. People are being motivated to give up the use of polythene. Most people have also started carrying cloth bags with them to buy vegetables and other things. People collect plastic waste and then sell it. With the revenue from waste, plastic recycling can also be done.

The corporation has already built its own waste manure units in gardens. Resident associations have also started this work in townships and colonies. It includes four bypass colonies. There are fertiliser units in more than 15 townships. Resident associations are also making compost from waste in some gardens. Apart from this, fertiliser is also being prepared in government schools. The corporation has also started marketing this organic manure, and farmers are being encouraged to buy it. At present, 900 tonnes of garbage are being released from the city. The corporation has set a target of reducing the volume of waste recycling and reuse to 200 tonnes a year. The corporation is also in touch with the business institutions of the city for this.

Reducing All Types of Pollution

In order to improve sanitation, work has begun to reduce pollution from noise, air, water. In addition, dust particles have been reduced in the atmosphere by 40%. In order to reduce water pollution, duct-taping is in progress.

□

8

The Impact of Media on Sanitation

The media of Indore city has always been ahead in arousing the awareness of the people of Indore. In the better management of their city, the media has speeded up its initiative as a part of the campaign.

During the planning of sanitation in Indore, the media took it upon themselves to initiate action. In the *Swachh Bharat Abhiyan*, the involvement and the role of the media in making Indore a clean city was remarkable.

Mediums involved: Newspapers, magazines, television, radio and social media; all mediums contributed to keeping Indore clean.

R.R. Patel, Joint Director, posted at Divisional Public Relations Office (Indore), says that the behaviour of the local media has been extremely sensitive and smooth towards their city. Together, everyone continuously undertakes positive initiatives to raise the prestige of their city and ensure Indore looks different from other cities.

This kind of approach on the media's part is rarely seen

in any other city. This is what the experience of Indore reveals. The media publishes all the sanitation-drive related news in Indore and runs a media literacy campaign among the people for awareness. From time to time, news is also published and broadcast to draw the attention of the administration. This kind of news does not come under a negative category but works towards coordination between the local public and administration. This important role of the media has helped make Indore the cleanest city in the country.

Senior journalist Navneet Shukla says that if you come to Indore, please take special care as you are in a clean and aware city. Keep the garbage in your pocket or dispose of it properly. If anyone is found littering, he or she has to pay for his or her illegal action.

Navneet Shukla says that the role of the media is important for the betterment, awareness and advancement of any city, state or country. Obviously, the media publishes those negative incidents and news daily, but it becomes our moral responsibility to make people aware of the betterment of our city. Today, we are talking about a clean Indore. Even before this, the media had campaigned for bringing Narmada water to Indore city for drinking purposes. Sanitation is the most important part of our better life. Yet, we have remained different and careless about sanitation due to a lack of true awareness. But the constant efforts to make people aware through media have made sanitation a part of the lifestyle of the people of Indore today. You will be surprised to know that if you do not correctly dispose of garbage, the people of Indore will correct you. The media has also played an important role in this lifestyle. You read in newspapers, magazines and watch TV, social media, and the hygiene camp, but every moment, the radio reminds you not to throw garbage.

Journalist Navneet Shukla narrates his experience that Indore has a different image when it comes to sanitation. Whether you are travelling or staying, your lifestyle will announce that you are from Indore city. Once on a train, we were all travelling with family members and eating food. After we had our food, all of us collected our own litter and wiped the area clean. Meanwhile, a member of our family came forward with a bag. Everyone disposed of their trash in that bag, and he went to the dustbin and deposited the trash neatly inside. This had become our habit, so nothing seemed different, but the other travellers watched us intently.

One of them did ask curiously, "Are you from Indore?" His question brought a smile on our faces. We said in unison – "Yes, we are from Indore." Now it was our turn to question.

We asked him, "Why did you suddenly say Indore?" His answer was equally splendid. "Every day, we read in newspapers, see on television that Indore is the number one city in the country in sanitation. Today, this attitude of you people helped us understand the reason behind Indore's number one journey." During the rest of the journey, we kept talking about the cleanliness of Indore. Ultimately, the good thing that happened is that those people too believed that sanitation is necessary for a healthy life. They said they too would maintain a clean environment around them.

Piyush Bhatt is a veteran journalist from Indore. He says that when Indore was associated with the *Swachh Bharat Abhiyan*, the challenge before all of us was how such a big city would be made clean. An even bigger question was how this childhood habit would be changed. But where there is a will, there is a way. The basic principle of media is broadcasting information, education and entertainment. The administration was also confident that the message of sanitation could reach people with the help of the media. It is the most powerful medium of communication. The administration discussed with media persons and sought their cooperation in this regard. With the administration's proposal being positive, favouring the city and its residents, the media too came on board. Articles were written in simple and common language.

In these articles, people were told about sanitation. Residents of Indore city were informed about *Swachh Bharat Abhiyan* and how our Indore city would be connected to it, and how we would become a clean city. The challenge was surely big but not so much that the media could not win the trust of the common public. Gradually, people supported the cause and today the result is visible to the entire world. The residents of Indore have changed their nature. Awareness has awakened in the people due to the activism of and help from the media.

Jitendra Jakatiya, who is doing a PhD in Indore's sanitation, says that the media did a lot of work. He says that while working with the media, he felt that he should do his doctorate on the subject of sanitation and cleanliness mission of Indore. Although it was not easy for him despite being a media person, he is slowly moving towards the result while working continually.

As a journalist, Jakatiya narrates his experience that the media is sensitising and energising the people of Indore and supporting the administration. Yet, where carelessness is seen in the administration, the media also works to caution them.

Jakatiya thinks that the wards where women workers work are cleaner than those wards where male employees work. It is because everyone works together that our Indore is consistently number one in sanitation.

In the context of women sanitation workers, Jakatiya says that cleanliness is more prominently found in women; sanitation is found everywhere where women work. No doubt, in the past years, Indore has done incredible work in the field of sanitation, and this was not possible without media participation and activism. Anyway, Indore's media has always been answerable to its city.

Young journalist Rashmi Jain says that our Indore is the role model for those cities and residents who wish to build strong awareness. With the participation of the administration and common people, Indore obtained the title of '*Swachh* Indore', also with the support of the media. We tried to bring the best side of Indore to the fore. It was also important that society considers what is published and broadcast in the media to be authentic. Our responsibility increases even more when we want to make people aware of our city having attained such a position. If we want to change the image of Indore, we have to write positive news. When you talk about positivity or positive behaviour, society too starts behaving the same way. However, when you take a negative direction, all positivity becomes blurred. The media has played a very positive role towards a clean Indore. The result of this today is that our Indore is consecutively at the number one position. We will all strive together that Indore should always remain number one in every aspect.

Senior journalist Jitendra Richharia says that another name for Indore's identity is positivity. It is not that Indore is different from other cities. In many ways, it is similar to other cities of the country, but one thing that makes it different from other cities is that for our Indore city, we shall all stand together.

The Government of India started the *Swachh Bharat Abhiyan*, and when the proposal for making Indore clean was presented, the media in Indore initiated the first move. The city's media drew the administration's attention to places where there was hindrance to Indore's sanitation or the areas in which there were the maximum obstacles.

The administration welcomed this initiative of the city's media and started working on the issues mentioned in the identified areas and preparing an action plan. After this, the media launched a campaign to make people aware of sanitation in the second phase.

Listening to the news and reading articles published in newspapers, programmes broadcast from radio and television, the awareness about cleanliness touched people's hearts and they gradually began cooperating. The administration's work was done smoothly. The media's initiative worked, and Indore began its sanitation drive.

The media of Indore became a voice for those people who were working towards sanitation in the second phase. They published the details of work done by the people along with their photographs in the newspapers. When success stories began to be published about the spirit of sanitation in them and the inspiration from which they started, people's interest increased further. People of every age group were working towards cleanliness. After publishing photos and names in newspapers, every resident of Indore had become the brand ambassador of the city's sanitation campaign. They felt proud calling themselves residents of Indore.

The administration also encouraged such people to come forward. The media played a big role in explaining the difference between wet and dry waste to people. New slogans were written. The media indeed did bear in mind that slogans and articles needed to be written, radio and television programmes created, all of which were intended to raise awareness among the people of Indore. Every person of Indore was happy that he/she was working for his/her city.

When Indore won the title of the first clean city in the

country in the *Swachh Bharat* Mission, the entire media was surprised at this news. Every politician and the common man realised that their hard work had paid off. Indore became a clean city. After attaining the status of a clean city for the first time, the people of Indore began working towards making their city cleaner with more vigour than before. Once again, the media was ready to cheer up the city. This series became an ongoing affair.

The media is constantly striving to keep Indore ahead in the *Swachh Bharat* Mission. Along with writing positive news, the media also publishes news whenever there occurs some carelessness or laxity. As in earlier instances, the administration neither ignores such news nor takes these reports in a negative way but based on them takes cognisance and corrects those deficiencies. The coordination of administration, civic, and Indore's media has changed the scenario of the city.

Journalist Rita Jain says that media has been a mirror of society since its birth. It publishes only those things that are for the betterment of society. It neither praises nor complains without reason. A clear example of this is the media in Indore. After the launch of the *Swachh Bharat* Mission, the role of media in the city has been commendable. Large media conglomerates to small newspapers and media institutions succeeded in creating the sense of 'Our Indore' in its people. The people of this city have a true love for it. Earlier, there was a traditional habit of carelessness among the people, and there was no place in their lifestyle for filth to be disposed of properly. Many crises happened. Even the media was unsure of how to inculcate the habit of hygiene and sanitation among the people.

Understanding its responsibility towards the society, the media also started publishing the news of activities happening during the events like Sanitation Week. But when it came to Indore's reputation in the *Swachh Bharat Abhiyan* and making it the best clean city in the country, the media took the first step. The media, which never published a single article regarding sanitation, unceasingly campaigned to create a cleaner Indore. That way, the media supported the sanitation drive in Indore.

In the process of creating awareness among the people in the campaign of *Swachh* Indore, the media started taking special care that people did not feel inferior about cleanliness. Instead, there should be a realisation in them that the mistakes they have done in the past would not be repeated. The initiative towards *Swachh* Indore became a campaign, and it was the media that first came forward. The media explained the meaning of cleanliness to the people. It created awareness among the people by talking to the doctors, discussing the work of voluntary organisations, and citing the efforts of the Municipal Corporation and the administration. Walking in and out of the house and in the city, people learnt and understood how to deal with garbage in public places.

Instead of accumulating waste inside the house, people kept two separate bins for collecting wet and dry waste. In the marketplace too, they made a habit of putting the waste in different compartments. Today, with the support of the media, Indore remains the cleanest city. Media is the strength of Indore and Indoris. There is usually criticism of social media being misused. Unnecessary things are posted, which does not benefit anyone but spreads confusion among the people, but the work that the Indoris did to make Indore clean with the help of social media is remarkable.

Vasundhara, 22, says that everything is not bad. What mindset you have and what you want to do are important. We are Indoris, and our love for Indore is pure. In such a case, if there is talk of making Indore clean, Indore as a brand ambassador in the *Swachh Bharat* Mission, the quickest and most powerful device of social media is available on everyone's palms. I wake up every morning and read the newspaper and re-write some of the news in my own way. My target is youth, so I make my point in their language. If the scenario of the entire country can be changed by running programmes such as Chai pe Charcha (discussion over a cup of tea) on social media, why can't the scenario of Indore be changed? Just with this thought, I kept posting three times a day separately.

Seeing those who shared my post and commented on them, I realised that even if I stood on the road and shouted my opinion, I could not have reached this audience. Today, in just five minutes, I am spreading my message to thousands of people. I am changing the way they think. Positivity is coming into their lives. Their thinking has started changing. Now before making a mess, they think and throw the garbage where it needs to be thrown. This is the power of social media.

People associated with me on social media say that they have changed their family's habits in their house. Roko started a campaign going from house to house. Almost every house has a box for dry and wet garbage. Despite that, the habit had not changed. The children and young members in the house not only continued to educate their elders but began implementing it themselves which led to a change in the habits of the rest of the family. I sometimes post some short videos in which people around me are inclined towards the cleanliness of Indore. I talk to them. They say when young children tell their mother, grandparents or other elder members, they also feel that the mistakes committed in the past should be corrected now. Social media has a big role to play along with other media, which we should use positively. If your one step has changed Indore, then you can change more cities.

Plastic Revolution

Today, the entire country is eulogising Indore for its remarkable success in sanitation. Earlier, it was a big challenge to collect and dispose of thousands of tons of garbage every day. Usually, the garbage was discarded at open places or vacant plots, and soon, a heap of garbage accumulated. Initially, the same thing happened with Indore, but when there is a problem, the people work to find a solution.

The administration did some phenomenal work in this direction, and gradually, mountains of garbage at many places in Indore vanished. Not only this, but the city also struck real gold from this waste in the form of organic manure. In making Indore beautiful, the administration also allowed the common people to earn from waste material. The journey from lack of cleanliness to sanitation was difficult. It was challenging, but the scenario has changed with well-planned efforts. You can understand it superficially, but if you study it deeply, you will realise how difficult and challenging it could be, and you wonder if it could have been possible. Yes, it is possible, and Indore has proved it.

The geographical area of Indore is 275 sq. km, and the population is over 30 lakhs. There are many historical and ancient places in parts of Indore, divided into 85 wards.

Apart from this, Indore is a traditional city despite being the state's commercial capital. Traditional festivals like Holi, Diwali, Eid, and Christmas are celebrated in Indore with enthusiasm and exuberance. There is an amazing variety of delicious foodstuffs available in the city. Initially, people of Indore had a bad habit of littering garbage like people elsewhere who are not conscious of maintaining cleanliness. There used to be a dustbin in houses, but it was only for namesake. The rest of the garbage was picked up and thrown elsewhere, expecting the Municipal Corporation staff would pick it up. Before the *Swachh Bharat Abhiyan*, like other Municipal Corporations, the modus operandi of the Indore Municipal Corporation was to collect the garbage once in two to four days. The Indore Municipal Corporation also had no roadmap for the disposal of the waste material.

It was collected at certain places. But the situation was the same on both sides. The residents were unaware, and the Municipal Corporation lacked sources and facilities. Generally, the budget of almost every municipality is the same, which is not enough to maintain hygiene in the city. Facilities and economic resources are limited. When Indore was included in the *Swachh Bharat Abhiyan*, the first challenge was collecting the garbage and the process of execution after its collection. The scenario started changing as soon as the *Swachh Bharat* Mission gathered momentum. In Indore, both people and authorities became aware, and consciousness began to awaken towards making the city clean, and the Municipal Corporation prepared its own roadmap for sanitation.

With 85 wards, Indore is today the most shining and sparkling city in terms of sanitation. More than five hundred garbage vehicles are collecting garbage from door-to-door. There is a system of collecting wet and dry waste separately in these garbage vehicles. One compartment is for wet waste and the other for dry waste. There is also another compartment in which biological and medical waste is dumped. Handcarts have also been arranged to collect wet and dry garbage from the narrow streets of Indore, where garbage vehicles are unable to reach. Later, it is put in the designated compartments in the garbage vehicle. Garbage vehicles collect waste from houses and reach their designated garbage transfer station, where wet and dry garbage is segregated into blue and green (20/16 Cubic Meter capacity capsule) containers. Wet waste of about 60 to 65 small vehicles is properly put into a green capsule and dry waste of about 40 to 45 small vehicles in a blue capsule.

It is transported to the trenching ground via truck through a hook loader. At the same time, biological organic waste is transferred to a different vehicle and sent to the biological medical waste disposal plant. The plant is located on Sanwer Road. In this plant, the ash remaining after incineration is transported to the company managing hazardous waste. Garbage collection is done once a day from the houses, which is sufficient given the amount of waste generated by the houses.

Secondly, there is a saving in human labour and material expenditure in collecting garbage from the houses once a day. But in commercial areas, garbage collection is done twice a day. At the same time, separate arrangements have been made for commercial establishments from which more than 10 kg of dry waste and 10 to 30 kg of wet waste are emitted daily. More than 61 dumpers and 17 compactors have been stationed to collect garbage from these places, and garbage is collected and transported directly to the trenching ground. More than three thousand twin litter bins have been installed in commercial areas for passers-by where the movement of people remains constant.

The wet and dry waste collected in all these twin litter bins is collected daily by special vehicles and emptied at their respective garbage transfer station. Feedback registers are also maintained at all the garbage collection vehicles to obtain suggestions and feedback from people regarding garbage collection. This register is inspected daily, and it is checked whether the performance of the vehicles which are engaged in garbage collection is perfect or not.

Immediate action is taken to address people's grievances. When someone wrote adverse comments, they were carefully considered, and if there was a fault in the system, then it was rectified. Not only this, but some suggestions also which were received were implemented to make Indore cleaner. Thus, in all 85 wards of Indore city, 100% segregated waste reaches the trenching ground with the help of a transfer station. An action plan has been made separately to ensure the training of drivers, monitoring by deputy sanitary inspectors, involvement of voluntary organisations, GPS in all vehicles, tracking and routing of vehicles to ensure they are working as per plan. The Indore Municipal Corporation has established an ISO certified workshop for GPS monitoring of vehicles and overall maintenance. The most remarkable thing is that this certified ISO workshop of the Indore Municipal Corporation is the only model of its kind in the country.

After the garbage is collected from houses and business places, it reaches the trenching ground. A weighbridge weighs the vehicles. The wet and dry waste is taken to the designated places and emptied. In this entire process, the wet waste is kept in the direction in which the wind blows so that the moisture of the wet waste is reduced. Along with this, drainage lines and leachate collection pits have also been arranged for the leachate that seeps into the soil from this wet waste. Bio-culture is periodically mixed and put into wet waste. At the same time, suitable spraying is also done to prevent the foul smell and the growth of bacteria that increases the composting process.

After 28 days of going through this entire process, this waste is transferred to the mechanical composting plant with a capacity of 600 MT per day for further processing. About 50 to 60 metric tons of compost is made daily from this waste. The agricultural scientists test the quality of this fertiliser in the lab built in the plant. After the testing of fertiliser to ensure that it is fully usable, permission is given for sale.

This fertiliser is sold at the rate of Rs.2 per kg in the open market under the brand name 'Indore City Compost'. The same fertiliser is sold in bags at the rate of Rs.3 per kg. The biggest customers of this fertiliser are farmers in and around Indore. Those who buy fertiliser include the Forest Department, Social Forestry, Indore Development Authority, the private nursery operators. There is also a system wherein every day, the complete information about the produce and sale of organic manure is uploaded by the Municipal Corporation on the M.F.M.S. portal of the Government of India. Transparency is maintained so that more people can get information about it. Dry waste is sent to the Material Recovery Centre 1 & 2 with 300/250 MT capacity per day.

Here, it is segregated by regulators. In dry waste, e-waste, metal, paper, glass, footwear and leather, cardboard products are given to companies for reuse. With the help of voluntary organisations, this work of recycling is handed over to authorised companies. Raw materials are made by processing polythene and the remaining plastic products at the plastic recovery centre. Plastic/polythene are also processed by various processors and then given for construction of asphalt roads, cement plants and pipe manufacturing factories.

Amino acids produced from hair waste generated from the city are manufactured in the plant set up by the Indore Municipal Corporation. Apart from this, the debris of broken buildings and new buildings in Indore city are useful for constructing pavers block in the C&D plant. In order to dispose of old waste of Indore city, the bio-remediation method has been completed to dispose of more than 2 million tonnes of old waste at the trenching ground at Devguradia. In this method, plastic, clay and inert etc. are separated from the old waste. Developing 100 acres of land by disposing of old waste and reclaiming the city forest is also in progress. Inert waste from processing wet and dry waste is being sent to a scientific engineered landfill site spread over about 2,600 acres.

After successful collection and disposal of waste, the process of decentralisation processing of waste is being ensured. The Municipal Corporation ensures that the organisations (residents associations, hotels and hospitals) generate more than 100 kilograms of waste daily by disposing of wet waste at the site. Organic waste converter machines, biogas plants or compost pits should be set up by which bio-fertiliser and biogas can be produced and used by them.

In the same process, waste coming out of 586 developed gardens owned by the Municipal Corporation of Indore is disposed of with the help of rag pickers. It is used to make manure from 368 compost pits established there.

Composting is done through peat. In this method, there is a system of disposal of waste from the temples. The process of manufacturing organic manure from the waste generated from the temples is going on uninterrupted. Similarly, a 20-tonne capacity biomethanation plant, 15-tonne capacity compost peat, and 15-tonne capacity biomethanation plant have been set up to dispose of waste originating from the Choithram vegetable market, Kabir Khedi. 1,400 kg of CNG gas is being made from this waste. Buses are running in Indore city with the help of CNG gas. On-site composting is being done by a drum composter machine with a 1ton capacity organic waste converter at

Nehru Park and Zoo in Indore city and a 25-ton capacity at Regional Park.

In the *Swachh Bharat* Mission, Indore has attained first place in sanitation thanks to the hard work of thousands of sanitation workers. More than 10,000 sanitation workers clean the residential areas every day.

At the same time, in the commercial areas, these sweepers are divided zone-wise, where cleaning is done thrice a day, and help is provided for collecting waste and transporting it to the destination. In Indore city, 500 kms road sweeping is done daily from 11 pm to 6 am with the help of a modern cleaning machine with mechanical cleaning. Apart from this, the footpaths and four lanes of the city are also cleaned by water through 12 pressure jet machines. The positive result of daily cleaning and sweeping is that the air quality of Indore city has started improving. Earlier, RSPM in the city was 140 micrograms per cubic meter, which has decreased to 76 micrograms per cubic meter.

Apart from vector-borne diseases, other diseases have also been controlled due to improvement in air pollution. The Indore Municipal Corporation takes special care that sanitation workers remain healthy. For this, the Corporation has given masks, jackets, gloves, two pairs of uniform, raincoats and shoes as items for personal protection to each sweeper. Aadhaar-linked biometric attendance has been made mandatory for all sanitation workers and their salaries are transferred to their bank accounts directly every month on time.

Monitoring of sanitation workers is done in association

with Health Officer, Chief Sanitation Inspectors (CSIs), Assistant CSIs, and voluntary organisations. The Municipal Corporation has fixed a fee for collection of garbage, where the residents are charged Rs.60 to Rs.150 per month, while the fee from commercial institutions is around Rs.150 to Rs.300 per month. Business institutions where 10 kg and more waste are generated are charged a waste management fee of Rs.450 to 45,000 per month. The waste management fee is managed from the amount received from user charges and property tax. Similarly, the Municipal Corporation levies charges for collection and transportation of garbage for wedding processions, rallies, events etc. A fine is levied for making the environment unclean, which ensures that the people maintain hygiene.

The fine ranges from a nominal amount of Rs.100 to a large penalty of Rs.1 lakh, and the penalty is charged immediately. According to an estimate, a penalty of about 1.25 crores was imposed in a year. By hiking the tax, the Municipal Corporation of Indore aims to increase its revenue collection and inculcate in people the habit of sanitation. Once they pay the penalty, they are more cautious the next time.

Experience tells that a person paying the fine becomes cautious and prevents people and family members from spoiling the environment. Once the people cultivate the habit of sanitation, they will think twice before spoiling the environment. Due to the various efforts of the administration, sanitation has become second nature of the people of Indore.

□

9

Testimonials—Indore of My Dreams

When it comes to Indore, every resident starting from the common man to the garbage collectors; everyone speaks in one voice. After Indore was crowned the cleanest city in the country, only one voice is heard from all sides that our Indore will continue to be an example of cleanliness. There will be no compromise on the cleanliness of Indore. People also believe that this new and beautiful face of Indore has emerged after the launch of *Swachh Bharat Abhiyan*. The Indoris have helped the city attain the number one place in *Swachh Bharat* Mission with the cooperation of the administration. There is only one sentence reverberating on people's tongues- this is the Indore of my dreams. 'This is the Indore of my dreams' is on everyone's lips.

Improvement in Climate

When the issue is about cleanliness, the leaders of Indore forget the political rivalry. BJP leader and former Mayor of Indore, Krishna Murari Moghe says that the status achieved by Indore in the matter of cleanliness has increased the value of every resident in the city. This habit has not only brought the diseases under control in the city but also improved the climate. Every person should take care of cleanliness, says Moghe. In fact, cleanliness has now become a part of the lifestyle of Indoris.

For instance, when we go outside Indore, our mind becomes restless when we see dirt somewhere. Why don't these people have any love for their city? Why are not these people conscious of cleanliness? However, I believe this happens due to lack of awareness. Indore is the city of my dreams, and today, the residents of clean Indore get appreciation, and their worth has increased, feels Moghe.

We Rise above Party Politics: Vinay Bakaliwal

Taking Moghe's point forward, Congress city president, Vinay Bakaliwal says that we rise above party politics when it comes to the development of Indore. First of all, we all belong to Indore. With the increase in the honour of Indore, our dignity also increases. When Indore topped in the *Swachh Bharat* Mission, not only one person, one party or one leader was happy, but all the Indoris had smiles on their faces because we all belong to the city of dreams. And when Indore remains at the forefront of cleanliness across the country, it is the collective success of all of us. I can say that we are seen with respect in other cities. When it comes to the betterment of the city, we don't involve party politics.

We are all the same in terms of cleanliness. Due to the cleanliness of Indore, many development works have been carried out in the city. We all gain from this. I am convinced that our first-generation too will always remain united for the development of Indore. We are taking this tradition forward, and the coming generation is also gearing itself and learning that there must be no politics which puts the development of Indore at stake. Together, we are making Indore a city of dreams, says Vinay Bakaliwal.

Common People are very Vigilant

From the politician to the common people, all are very alert towards their dream city Indore. Abhilasha Patil, a housewife who lives in Kalani Nagar, says that the number one position of Indore in cleanliness means that our dreams are coming true. She said that the cleanliness drive has instilled in us a habit of keeping our homes clean. No one has to tell us about keeping wet and dry waste separately in the house. Every member of the family understands his/her responsibility and puts wet and dry waste in separate bins. As soon as the garbage vehicle arrives, all the people dump the household garbage in the vehicle. This keeps the colony clean, says Abhilasha.

Vasundhara Dangi, a housewife who lives in Indrapuri, said that there are many hostels in and around the houses in our colony. When children from outside cities see the cleanliness here, they start cleaning their rooms and surroundings. They don't even throw trash on the road. This pleasant change has been possible ever since Indore has been named the cleanest city in the country for the fifth consecutive time. Earlier, we had to do a lot of explaining to the children who came from outside. We had to persuade them to maintain cleanliness. But now, this is not necessary. Now, they have started understanding their responsibility. The children feel that it is their responsibility to keep the city of their dreams clean, says Vasundhara.

Shyam Verma, who uses public transport, says that he was always disturbed by the wrappers of peanut and gutkha, etc., lying everywhere, but now everyone understands their responsibility, and the wrappers of all these items are thrown in the dustbins. Indore is an example for the whole country in maintaining cleanliness. That is why we say that Indore is not just a city but a city of our dreams. Verma further says that many people even keep the waste with them while travelling, and when they get off the bus, they put it in the garbage boxes which the Municipal Corporation has installed. This habit distinguishes the people of Indore from the people of other cities, and for this reason, their identity is also different from others.

Rupali Singh, who travels in a local city bus, says now that people of Indore have adopted clean habits, and will not give them up. Earlier, they had to be motivated and persuaded. This change did not come in a day; rather, it is the outcome of sustained efforts, and those who did not listen were penalised as well as convinced. Today, all the big temples also have a good system of cleanliness in place. It motivates people to be responsible.

Nitin Verma, a teacher in a school in the city, says that the habit of cleaning should be developed in the children from the beginning. This is the time to make children responsible towards their city. I am happy that we are moving in this direction. Earlier, we used to tell the children to maintain cleanliness around them. However, as Indore moved towards becoming the country's cleanest city, we do not need to teach the children about cleanliness. They do the cleaning on their own. The children even plead with those who do not maintain cleanliness around their houses. According to Nitin, this pleasant change makes the city number one in the country in terms of cleanliness.

Bhavesh Joshi, a teacher at the Vivekananda School, says that earlier during the period of moral education in the schools, we used to tell children about the importance of hygiene. But you do not need that now because the children themselves maintain sanitation. They incorporate the importance of cleanliness in their daily lives. And for this reason, Indore remains number one in the country. The Municipal Corporation has also done a lot of work and tried to make people responsible. We all feel that as the name of Indore becomes better well-known in the country, our dreams will come true, and we will be able to say that we are the proud residents of Indore.

Shyam Rao, who works as a watchman at an ATM in Indore city, says people have become more aware of cleanliness. Initially, customers used to discard the renewal tabs on the floor while coming out of the ATM, but they now put them in the garbage can. And when they don't see any bins, they come and question why the bins are not provided. This change and sense of responsibility sets Indore apart from other cities and always puts it on the top of the country's list in terms of cleanliness. Shyam Rao says that this is the beginning of making our dream come true.

Agreeing with his views, a watchman in a multi-storey building, Gulab Singh says that earlier people used to spit the residue of paan, betel nut, tobacco etc. in the multi-storey building, but now the Municipal Corporation has made strict rules to end this bad habit. And they have also fined some people. This has brought about a change as people are now learning to give up their habit of spitting here and there. And this made it much easier to clean the buildings. This very spirit of cleanliness sets apart the people of Indore from the rest of the country, and that is why the city has retained the title of the cleanest city for the fifth time in a row.

Babu Dilip Singh Sikarwara at the collectorate said that the collector pays a lot of attention to cleanliness. Hence, people who work under him also have to be careful. The collectorate complex is always clean. All of us also put the waste papers in the garbage bags. People coming here for their work also do not throw the garbage and make use of the dustbin. This was not the situation in the past. Pieces of paper could be seen scattered everywhere. Moreover, the people who came here for work also had the habit of spitting after chewing *paan, gutkha* etc. Now they have given up this habit.

This has brought about significant improvements, and

the entire campus looks spick and span. The Collectorate Complex here is very clean compared to its counterparts in other cities. Here, the employees engaged in cleaning worked very hard. They say that they cannot get complete success by cleaning only some areas of the city. This is the dedication with which Indorians have presented Indore as the model of cleanliness before the whole world, opines Babu Dilip Singh. No one tells us to maintain hygiene anymore; they do not need to. Yes, whenever there is a need to tell anyone, one can be sure that he/she is not from the city of our dream Indore.

Sepoy Dilip Raghuvanshi from the Sanctuary police station says that the dedication of the people of Indore is very remarkable. First, there was a lack of awareness among the masses, but people became conscious and aware after Indore became number one. This is the reason that cleanliness has become a habit of the people. Indore's cleanliness is our pride as well as responsibility. After all, we have a separate place and identity in the country. At other places, people often have to be taught how important it is to maintain hygiene, although sanitation drives are being conducted constantly.

TI NS Raghuvanshi says that Indore's cleanliness is motivating people living in the villages and outskirts. They have now undertaken cleaning drive on their own. There has been a big change. People have realised that keeping the diseases at bay ultimately saves a lot of money. Indore is our pride and identity. We are all responsible residents; we will take it forward, says Raghuvanshi.

Gandalal, who has a shop selling *golgappas* on the

roadside at Zanjeer's crossroads, says that like *golgappe*, my Indore is now very beautiful. Due to cleanliness, we can do our business conveniently and easily. Earlier, there was a problem finding a clean place to sell because people hesitated to eat *golgappas* as the surroundings were dirty. Now this problem has been solved because every crossroad of the city, every street and *mohalla* is clean. The campaigns for cleaning have also made people like us responsible. Roadside vendors have to keep a garbage box near the handcart on which they sell food items. This does not allow the dirt to spread. Due to cleanliness, we can save ourselves from many diseases.

Baseralal Meena, who is settled in Indore, says public awareness very much impacts the city's cleanliness. He always maintains cleanliness and keeps reminding his customers to keep the area clean and put the garbage in the garbage compartment. Meena says it is a pleasant feeling to work in clean surroundings.

Mohammed Nasir, who worked near the Robot intersection on Ring Road, says that earlier people used to stock old junk items at their homes. This junk was not only unclean but also caused disease and proved harmful to the environment. But now the thinking of people has changed. Due to the increasing awareness among the people towards cleanliness, they sell the junk goods thus benefitting junk dealers like Nasir. People have stopped keeping old stuff in their homes. Now there is no difficulty in segregating paper, iron, and plastic accessories. But earlier, we had to separate the junk and had to employ a man for this work. This has also increased our savings. Also, it is easy to collect junk from the garbage stations. Many times, we get ten quintal junk in one day. All this has happened due to the cleanliness drive in the city. Nasir says that our work is to keep the houses and the city clean. Now that change has come, it makes us happy. After all, Indore is ours.

Eighty-year-old Pushpa Bakaliwal's house is near the bypass. She always had trouble breathing due garbage burning in the trenching ground. It used to be difficult to get out of the house, but now she goes out of the house both in the morning and evening. This has been possible due to the cleanliness in the trenching ground. She says I am relieved now as the air is clean and there is no smoke.

Babulal Sharma, 72, has been a police officer living in the Tilak Nagar area of the city. He was disturbed by the city's dust, due to which he could not even go for a walk, but now he regularly goes for morning walks. He says he has the habit of staying fit but was troubled by dust as it caused allergy. Now he can freely walk on the roads too. This beautiful change happening in his city has given him a new life.

Kalpana Chauhan, a housemaid lives in a multi-storey building located at the Bengali crossroads on the second floor. Earlier, due to dust and smoke from the vehicles, she had to clean the house all the time, which made her agitated, but now she is relieved because the machines clean the dust from the roads every night. Kalpana says that she is willing to do whatever it takes in keeping Indore clean because it is not about cleanliness alone, but the reputation of Indore which is also at stake. And when it comes to Indore, how can we stay behind?

While agreeing with Kalpana, Kiran Yadav says that we thank the *Swachh Bharat* Mission for teaching us to be clean. The campaign has made Indore clean and has inculcated a feeling of belongingness among the people towards their city. Kiran Yadav's house is in a multi-storey building on AB Road. She was always busy cleaning her house. This affected her health. Even after spending a lot of money on her treatment, she did not get any relief. Now this problem has been resolved now since the dust from the roads does not enter the house.

For Class X student Paritosh Kaushik, clean Indore is a big achievement for him. He is happy that the *Swachh Bharat* Mission has changed the picture of Indore. Paritosh, a schoolboy who rides a bicycle, says that his school uniform had to be washed every day because of the dust on the roads. The rainy season was particularly troublesome because the mud spoiled the clothes. He was in a dilemma every day as the uniform did not dry up quickly, but now there was no need to worry about washing it every day.

Similarly, another student Suchitra has got rid of many kinds of problems as the city is now clean and there is no filth and dirt, no heaps of rotting garbage. She is also happy that her own city Indore has been included in the country's most beautiful and clean city. She says that she used to read about the city of dreams in books and stories, but now it is coming true. Recalling the past, Suchitra Dewangan, a student, studying in class 12th, says that her school is on the main road. Continuous movement of vehicles all day caused respiratory problems due to dust pollution. It used to be difficult even to sit in class during the winter season, but now due to cleanliness, there is no dust which lets them study peacefully

Rajni Bhandari, a writer said that the environment in the country's cleanest city, Indore, has changed rapidly. Indore has worked in every area, from cleanliness on the roads to the disposal of waste, which has led to this improvement. We had never even imagined that our Indore could be so clean and beautiful. But now it is a reality on the ground. Indore is the cleanest city in the country.

Dinkar Bhandari, a poet said that he used to have persistent eye problems due to the dust, but now things are much better. He has no eye problem now. Dinkar says that the *Swachh Bharat* Mission has given Indore a new name and new identity. Today, we can proudly say that Indore, called Mini Bombay, is recognised as a Big Clean City, not a Mini City. This success of Indore is a matter of pride for people like me, says Bhandari.

Gurmeet Chawla, operator of an electronic equipment showroom located on AB Road, says that the showroom had to be cleaned throughout the day due to dust. There was a fear of malfunction of the equipment due to dust. Now the problem is over as the roads are cleaned and washed at night. The business has become easier and smooth, and when I see the success of Indore on television, I feel overjoyed. We have taken the responsibility for cleanliness, and even during our family functions at home, we take proper care to keep our surroundings clean. Earlier, attention was paid only towards making arrangements for food and drink. Now a team is deployed to ensure that there is no mess. Gurmeet says that these small efforts of ours help the sanitation workers. Their time is also saved, giving them more time to clean other places.

Gaurav Ranadive, BJP President of Indore city said that the city's climate has considerably improved due to the cleanliness drive. AE Dinesh Jain of Indore Pollution Control Board said that the Pollution Control Board issued monthly reports of all 51 districts. In this list, Indore has always stayed below 35, despite Indore being the industrial capital of the state. Environmentalist GD Agarwal said that the officers from other cities in the country also visited Indore to see what was being done in the city to save the environment.

The municipal authorities had started cleaning the city's roads to reach the number one place in cleanliness. Every night, the main roads of the city are cleaned with machines. This led to a dust-free city. At the same time, the diseases caused by dust have largely disappeared. All the dirt from the city has vanished. It had a direct impact on health. Trenching Ground was the biggest problem in Devgurdia. The people living in the 5 km radius were always complaining about cough and respiratory problems. Earlier, in the city, plastic bags were used very regularly. The workers used to burn them in the open. It spread poisonous smoke and made people sick, but now it does not happen. The river flowing through the city remains clean. Plantation has been done on the banks of the river. Dirty settlements around the river are no longer dirty, and the health of the people has improved.

Dr. Sharad Pandit, the main medical officer at Maharaja Yashwant Rao Hospital in Indore, says that a hygienic and clean atmosphere has made people healthier. Diseases caused by dirt and filth have decreased a lot.

In order to take stock of this situation, the Indore Municipal Corporation surveyed the city's doctors, drug associations, Indian Medical Association. According to Dr. A. D. Bhatnagar, Chief Health Officer, the number of patients suffering from diseases like vomiting, diarrhoea, hepatitis, malaria, dengue, etc., has significantly declined. Earlier, about 1,000 patients used to visit the OPD every day to get treatment for these diseases. But now, only around 35,000 visited the hospitals in the last quarter.

Madhusudan Mandloi, a doctor in the district hospital, said that now fewer people fall sick in Indore due to good hygiene. The supply of free drugs from the hospital has declined by 15 per cent. At the same time, in the last three months of COVID-19, no person died in Indore from dengue. Due to cleanliness, the quality of air has improved a lot. Due to this change, people's resistance to diseases is also improving.

Dr. Sanjay Londhe, President of the Indore Medical Association, said that Indore has achieved the goal of better health. During summer and monsoons, crowds of patients could be seen in government hospitals and private clinics. But now the people are healthier. Cleanliness has contributed towards better health of the people and decline in diseases.

Vinay Bakaliwal, President of Indore Chemist Association, said that the sale of medicines to treat the diseases of liver and dehydration declined by 70 percent. The Health Officer of the Indore Municipal Corporation, Dr. Uttam Yadav, said that many doctors and hospitals have confirmed that the overall health of the people has improved, and surveys have revealed a decline in the sale of some medicines. He said that the results of the drive for sanitation are now visible.

Indore has been number one in the country in cleanliness for the fifth consecutive time. There is a great contribution of the municipal employees and the people behind this. The cleaning of the city would not have been possible without their cooperation. It inspires people to love their city. Due to the honest efforts for cleanliness, Indore continues to be an example for the country. Every class of the city is happy with the cleanliness. Sanitation workers have also been hailed and appreciated all over the country. They get uniforms with reflective radium tape which helps them clean the roads at the night. As they wear gloves and other protective equipment, the risk of infection has decreased.

□

10
Door to Door Collection

The Solid Waste Management Rules 2016 defines Municipal Solid Waste (MSW) as the waste consisting of everyday items such as product packaging, grass clippings, furniture, clothing, bottles and cans, food scraps, newspapers, appliances, consumer electronics, and batteries. Municipal solid waste is generated from various sources such as households, commercial establishments, educational institutions, etc.

In 2014, the Ministry of Housing and Urban Affairs, Government of India launched the *Swachh Bharat* Mission (Urban) that made it mandatory for all Urban Local Bodies (ULB) to ensure 100% door to door collection of MSW, along with source segregation of waste in at least two categories, i.e. dry waste and wet waste.

Prior to 2015, the IMC lacked any proper mechanism for collecting and transportation of the MSW generated in the city. The city was characterised by several open dump sites, Garbage Vulnerable Points (GVPs) and secondary storage bins that were rarely emptied. However, in 2015, the IMC resolved to transform the then-existing deplorable conditions, and since then, it has not only implemented 100% door to door collection but also successfully implemented source segregation of waste.

Collection Mechanism Deployed by the IMC

The IMC has over 700+ vehicles assigned in the collection and transportation of MSW from the source or point of generation to the endpoint or processing facility. After careful deliberations, it has devised a strategy to ensure 100% deployment of the vehicles on predetermined routes, with unique beats and a fixed number of workers for every vehicle. All vehicles are tracked through GPS-enabled tracking system and Push to Talk (PTT) devices via the IMC's unique control room. The IMC has set up a workshop for the repairs and maintenance of all the vehicles deployed in the city. Additionally, the vehicles are also governed by a fuel management system. Every morning, the vehicles are refuelled and tracked throughout the day based on the distance travelled and fuel utilised.

Six Types of Source Segregation

In 2020, through extensive IEC drives and capacity building of staff and field workers, the IMC successfully introduced six types of waste segregation. Irrespective of bulk or non-bulk waste generators, all waste generators segregate their waste in the following six categories as (i) Plastic Waste—includes dry waste that comprises of plastic such as plastic bottles, cutlery, plastic containers etc. (ii) Non- Plastic Waste—includes all other types of dry waste (excluding those comprising of plastic) elements such as paper, cardboard, metal, glass etc. (iii) Wet Waste—biodegradable waste primarily originating from the kitchen such as vegetable and fruit peels, leftover food scraps, meat and fish bones etc. (iv) Domestic Hazardous Waste—includes discarded paint drums, CFL bulbs, tube lights, broken mercury thermometers, used batteries etc. (v) Sanitary Waste—primarily includes menstrual waste and diapers (vi) Electronic Waste—includes electronic appliances such as refrigerators, machines, fans, air conditioners, hair dryers, irons, watches, mobile phones etc.

From Source to Garbage Transfer Stations

The IMC has deployed vehicles to collect and transport waste from source to garbage transfer stations and, finally, to the processing facilities. The action plan adopted for the door-to-door collection and transportation of all types of waste from various waste generators is that the segregation of waste is carried out from the source to the endpoint, i.e., processing facility.

Door to Door Collection (Non-Bulk Waste Generators)

All households, commercial and other establishments daily generating less than 50 kgs of MSW come under this category. All units falling in this category segregate their waste into six categories. The vehicles deployed for door-to-door collection of waste are primarily partitioned open tippers, e-rickshaws etc., broadly divided into wet and dry waste (non-plastic). There is a separate bag for plastic waste, and the other three remaining waste are collected in three separate smaller bins attached to the vehicles. The IMC also encourages households to practice on site composting. For door-to-door collection of waste from non-bulk waste generators, two types of vehicles are used- open tippers and compartmentalised tippers.

Litter Bins Waste Collection

The IMC has over 3,074 twin litter bins installed in public, commercial and other identified areas with high footfall. The IMC has 107 dedicated open tippers for the collection of waste from the litter bins.

From Transfer Station to Processing Facilities

On arrival, first, the RFID id is tagged and then sent to the weighbridge for weighing the MSW transported. Three smaller bins are offloaded, weighed and recorded. Then the bag carrying plastic waste is weighed and recorded. Thereafter, the total remaining dry and wet waste is recorded. Finally, the weight of the vehicle is recorded. An Integrated Online System is used to monitor real-time activities of the vehicles as well as the Transfer Stations. The Control Room keeps a check on the amount of waste reaching the 10 Transfer Stations, the amount of waste processed every day to ensure that MSW reaching the Transfer Station does not exceed its capacity.

The segregated MSW is then transferred to the designated centralised processing facilities

Wet Waste- The wet waste is then transferred to Centralised Wet Waste Processing Facilities such as the Biomethanation Plant at Kabit Khedi and Waste to Compost Plant at Devguradiya Trenching Ground.

Dry Waste (Both Plastic and Non-Plastic)—The Dry waste is sent to Centralised Material Recovery Facilities (MRF) of the IMC. The IMC has two facilities-the first is an automated MRF, and the second is manual MF, wherein manually further segregation, recycle and reuse is carried out.

E-Waste—The collected e-waste is sent to the IMC's empanelled agency Unique Eco-recycle, an authorised e-waste recycler registered with the Madhya Pradesh Pollution Control Board.

Domestic Hazardous Waste—The collected Domestic Hazardous Waste is sent to Pithampur Industrial Waste Management Private Limited (Ramky), an authorised processor of DHW and under contract with the IMC.

Sanitary Waste—The collected sanitary waste is sent to Eco Pro Environmental Services for scientific and safe disposal. It is an authorised processor of sanitary waste.

Bulk Waste Generators

Bulk Waste Generators (BWGs) are broadly categorised into two categories between 10 to 50 kgs and above 50 kg. For BWGs generating MSW above 50 kgs, only plastic, non-plastic and the other three categories of waste is collected, while wet waste is processed on site. In the case of BWGs generating MSW between 10-50 kgs, the IMC collects both dry and wet waste and all other categories of waste from the IMC. The vehicles directly transfer the waste to the Processing Facilities through compactors. At present, there are 287 BWGs in the city.

The IMC has designated vehicles to collect the waste from meat and fish vendors in the city. The waste is collected directly from the source and taken to the processing facility.

Monitoring Mechanism

The IMC has devised a strategic plan to keep a check on the collection mechanism in the city at three levels:

Ward Level

At the ward level, the NGO teams accompany the door-to-door collection of MSW from the households. During the collection, they keep a check on segregated waste given by the residents and assist in case the segregation is not done in a requisite manner. Secondly, the vehicles are checked once they arrive with the collected waste at the Garbage Transfer

Stations (GTS), where logbooks are maintained real-time. In case segregation standards are not met, or mixed waste is found, then the concerned Daroga is contacted with the help of the Control Room, and MSW is properly segregated. In the case of repeat offenders, disciplinary action is taken against the concerned personnel in the form of salary cuts. Additionally, digital tools such as Collection and Segregation App are also used to check the MSW collected.

City Level

At the city level, the IMC has two Material Recovery Facilities for dry waste processing operated and maintained by Nepra and Human Matrix Solutions for 400 TPD Waste to Compost Plant for processing wet waste. Both facilities keep a holistic check on the incoming MSW and notify the concerned *Darogas* and officials.

Role of Indore's Residents

The residents of Indore play a key role in maintaining the city's SWM system in check. The IMC has its own Indore 311 app, which is very actively used by the city residents. The residents use the app to share any concerns and seek assistance, if required, for source segregation.

The IMC's elaborate yet carefully designed deployment of the door to door vehicle system enables it to ensure that the city is clean without any dump sites and vulnerable garbage points and maintains its status of bin free city.

□

11

Plastic-Free Initiative of Indore

Plastics constitute a growing threat to our environment—and in turn, human well-being—affecting the world's freshwater systems and marine resources in particular, as well as terrestrial biodiversity and public health.

Indore has been taking many initiatives to reduce the use of single-use and throwaway plastics. In the last four years, all types of single-use plastics and disposable plastic items under the 3 R initiatives of Indore have been completely banned.

The IMC has done extensive awareness campaigns in all the 85 wards to acquaint the public at large about the negative impacts of single-use plastics in day-to-day life and has provided information about the availability and use of alternate products to reduce single-use plastic and support the IMC in making Indore a plastic-free city.

Under the 3 R initiatives, the IMC has introduced many measures like collection and purchase of segregated plastic at the household level, Bartan Bank to eliminate disposable plastic material, Jhola bank to eliminate single-use plastic carry bags, Plastic EPR Indore Action Plan for partial cost recovery of plastic collection and processing, BYR in the city to encourage all residents, government and private offices, educational institutions, commercial establishments to adopt the 3R principles by making and using their own reusable steel kit, Plastic premier League PPL for creating awareness and collection of segregated waste plastic, zero waste wards and colonies and disposal free markets.

The Plastic Waste Collection System

The Indore Municipal Corporation has introduced a separate plastic waste collection system. IMC collects all kinds of plastic waste through its authorised vehicles in a special bag given by Corporation. Plastic carry bags (more than 50 microns), milk pouches, water bottles, discarded buckets, mugs, tetra-packs, pens, and plastic packaging are collected from residents in segregated form. In return for the plastic waste, residents are paid Rs. 1.5 per kg.

The non-recyclable plastic waste collected with dry waste at the household level goes to the material recovery facility. Dry waste is divided into different categories like paper, cardboard, plastic, metal, and others at the material recovery facility. Thus, plastic waste is converted into plastic pellets if reusable and non-usable plastic is sent to cement plants for disposal.

Indore has set up a robust system for managing plastic waste and has shown others how plastic can be effectively managed. Over the years, the IMC has introduced several innovative measures for plastic waste reduction in the city.

Processing of Plastic Waste

To handle and process dry waste, IMC has developed 2 Material Recovery Facilities at Devguradiya Trenching Ground. One facility is a state-of-the-art 300 TPD fully automatic Material Recovery Facility developed on a PPP basis and a 200 TPD semi-automatic material recovery facility.

A plastic processing plant is established at these material recovery facilities. About 80 to 100 TPD plastic is recovered at the material recovery facility. The reusable plastic is segregated and processed. The recyclable low density polythene (plastic bags) gets cleaned and recycled in a *gatta* plant, where the plastic pellets are sold to irrigation pipe manufacturers. The non-recyclable plastic is sent to the cement plant for disposal.

Revenue through the implementation of Extended Producers Responsibility:

Indore has become the first city in India to ink a pact with producer responsibility organisations (PROs) authorised by the MP Pollution Board for disposing of plastic waste. Under the Plastic Waste Management Rules 2016, Indore Municipal Corporation has signed a contract with these PROs authorised by the MP Pollution Board where part of the cost incurred in collection, transportation and treatment of plastic waste is recovered.

For plastic waste management, the Central government had notified the Plastic Waste Management (PWM) Rules 2016. These rules have been applied to every manufacturer of plastic, its importer and all the institutions that are recycling brands (PIBO) in India. Under these rules, the brand owners/producers are required to bear the cost of plastic utilised in their products. PR acts as a link between the urban bodies for disposal of plastic waste disposed of by the manufacturer of plastics, its importer and the brand owner (PIBO).

IMC estimates a revenue of about Rs. 60 lakh per annum from the EPR initiative, which will be utilised in waste plastic management.

There are unique 3 R initiatives of the IMC for Plastic reduction and Plastic Free Indore Bartan Bank. Since 2019, the IMC has introduced Bartan Banks in the city. As the name suggests, the banks provide steel utensils like plates, bowls, glasses, spoons etc., free of cost to the people to discourage using single-use disposables and keep the city clean, litter-free and plastic disposable free. To avail the services of the Bartan Banks, the residents place a request through Indore 311 App that directs them to the nearest Bartan.

The desired number of utensils is provided free of cost, on the condition that no disposable item is used in the event or occasion. The crockery is then to be cleaned up and returned to the Bank. In case utensils are damaged or lost, then the issuer is charged to recover the cost. Additionally, through the Indore 311 App, the residents can also donate utensils to the Banks.

The introduction of Bartan Banks has had a considerable impact on the city, such as prevention of single-use disposables such as plastic or thermocol, prevention of littering, awareness of residents about the harmful effects of single-use disposable items and acquainting the residents towards adopting 3R principles in daily lives.

Jhola/Thaila Bank

In lieu of its ban on single-use plastic and encourage the use of alternatives, the IMC has introduced Jhola Banks in the city that provides reusable cloth bags and paper bags at a minimal price to the residents. The first Jhola Bank was inaugurated on 2nd October 2019, i.e., the 150th birth anniversary of Mahatma Gandhi.

The Jhola banks partnered with local Self-Help Groups to make the *thailas* for the banks. The raw material used to make the *thailas* was from old clothes donated from residents or collected during door-to-door collection of waste. The novelty of the initiative was that it not only helped to discourage residents from using single-use plastic bags but also provided income-generating opportunities to the women of the SHGs, paving the way for women's economic empowerment. In order to incentivise the usage of *thailas* from Jhola Banks, the IMC regulated the prices of the bags such that the rate of the *thailas* was lower rates than the market prices.

The Jhola Banks have had significant impacts on the IMC. Most importantly, they have facilitated the successful elimination of single-use plastic bags in the city. The Jhola banks have helped the IMC to raise awareness about the harmful effects of plastic and encouraged residents to adopt 3R principles in their daily lives.

Disposable Free Markets are another initiative that aimed to eliminate single-use plastic disposables in commercial and public areas, especially with heavy footfall. Awareness drives were conducted in popular markets such as Sarafa Bazaar, 56 Dukaan and Meghdoot Gardens that generated vast amounts of disposable plastic waste to discontinue the practice. Meetings with market associations and shopkeepers were conducted to motivate them not to use plastic and thermocol disposables and use alternatives like steel.

The financial benefits of making the switch to the durable alternative were explained, which made the initiative more lucrative and popular. The city's major markets that have adopted the practice include 56 Dukan, Sarafa Market, Meghdoot Gardens, 54 Market, Anand Bazaar, Bhol Nath Ustad, etc.

For successful implementation, the markets encourage their customers to bring their reusable bags or *jholas* from home, or if needed, provide carry bags that are either above 50 microns in thickness or made from cloth or other recycled items. The alternate bags are sold at a price to motivate the customers to bring their own reusable bags from their homes and inculcate positive practices in their everyday lives.

Bring Your Recyclables (#BYR)

IMC has launched the unique initiative of Bring Your Recyclables or #BYR in the city to encourage all residents, government and private offices, educational institutions, commercial establishments to adopt 3R principles by making and using their own recyclable kit. The special recyclable kit was made of a recycled cloth bag comprised of one glass, spoon, bowl and bottles.

The vision behind the initiative was that the cloth bag would be an eco-friendly alternate in place of plastic bags that the residents could use whenever they stepped out or for daily use. The spoon, glass and bowl would serve as an alternative for single-use disposables, viable options to maintain good health and hygiene as well as prevent littering in public and commercial areas. Finally, the bottles would avert the significant plastic waste arising from plastic water bottles found in commercial and public areas, offices and institutions.

Plastic Premier League

This year (2020), the IMC launched a unique one-of-its-kind initiative called Plastic Premier League (PPL) to discourage using single-use plastic products. The IMC formed four teams with local celebrities associated with cricket and Radio Jockey's (RJs) working in the city for the initiative. The IMC lent support to the teams by providing five vehicles and workers to each team to help them collect the single-use plastics from their respective areas. The PPL was conducted between 20th October to 31st October, i.e., for a period of 45 days, and the winning team was awarded the PPL Trophy.

For the initiative, the teams conducted awareness drives to discourage plastic usage, encourage the use of alternatives such as cloth *thailas,* etc. The teams also organised Plastic Walks and hosted digital campaigns on social media to encourage maximum participation from the residents. Additionally, the IMC also operated 19 special vehicles in each of 19 zones in the city to collect plastic waste from the households and commercial establishments in the city.

□

12

Indore Rajwada and Chhappan Dukan

The essence of Indore is completely different from other cities. Time is a regular factor in all other cities from sunrise to sunset, but if we talk about Indore, life here is out of the ordinary. It is simple and sweet, and people enjoy every moment of their existence, and the day is not just spent but well spent. Time has its own significance in the life of an Indori. Every day is like a festival. With the rising of the sun, the city wakes up after night's slumber, and people can be seen greeting each other with *Ram-Ram Bhaiya*, but as the day draws towards a close, the energetic and charismatic voice of a DJ will help you forget all your concerns and relax.

People of Indore are foodies at heart, and restaurants and roadside vendors serve the yummiest traditional food and exotic dishes from other parts of the country. A cup of steaming tea with *poha* welcomes you in the morning, followed by a busy and bustling life at Rajwada in the afternoon and an inevitable visit to the famous Chappan

Dukan in the evening where delicious and appetising dishes are waiting for you. The lives of the Indoris do not stop here.

The festive atmosphere prevailing from dawn to dusk in the magnificent city of Indore makes it stand out amongst all other cities. The day begins with the spiritual hymns imparting tranquillity, and the people end their day with full zeal. Indorians are fun-loving. They love to live life to the fullest. They believe in working hard and partying harder. They believe that the day might have ended, but life must go on with gusto and passion.

Indore is a foodie's paradise. The city has an umpteen variety of deliciously prepared lip-smacking dishes to suit one and all taste buds. From twilight, the air is filled with the steam of piping hot tea and *poha*–Indorians' favourite breakfast, from the small stalls of the roadside vendors. By noon, the streets are full of the hustle and bustle of cars, buses and bikes, along with individuals of all ages. Every person moves towards chasing his goals, and as the dusk sets in, life takes a pleasant break with a nibble and munch of spicy *chaats* with sweet and savoury *chutney* and other delicacies at Chhappan Dukan.

As the night sets in, the luminance and radiance of the streets of Sarafa Bazaar are bewildering. As the jewel merchants shut their stores and prepare to head home, the local chefs are all set to amaze the food lovers with mouth-watering delicacies like *bhutte ka kees* and *khopra* patties, *shikanji, mawa baati, jalebi, kulhad wali chai,* and the list goes on...

The night food market of Sarafa Bazaar hosts thousands of people daily. Flocks of people head towards the Sarafa Food Bazaar at night to have fun and delectable food. A notable thing amongst all this cram of thousands of people is that no one argues with anyone. It's a happy and peppy atmosphere. It is impressive to note that not even a speck of thrash or scrap of wastepaper is tossed on the ground. No person can be seen littering the surroundings. It has become a tradition of these responsible Indoris to maintain the freshness and purity of their city. It seems these people have imbibed the lesson of cleanliness and neatness into their hearts and souls. It is commendable to see such a large mob eating together without messing up the place. It is astounding to note that these Indoris are well aware of the tidiness and sanitation of their city from daybreak to wee hours.

Indore has been voted the cleanest city for five years in a row. This awareness and good mannerism of the common man has a huge role to play in keeping the city so clean and tidy. But it hasn't always been like this -. Since the city came into existence, the people here loved food, but the tradition to take up cleanliness as a religious habit is a new concept. Four years back, the *Swachh Bharat Abhiyan* gripped my attention when I was the city's collector, and I, along with the city municipal commissioner Manish Singh decided that a city like Indore, which is ahead of many cities in all aspects, must take an oath to leap forward in cleanliness as well. Initially, it was not easy to change the notion towards waste. But the hard work and efforts of the administration paid off, and Indore managed to bag the Clean City award five times in a row. This success was due to the meticulous efforts of the administration as well as the passion of the people towards their city.

As the day's routine comes to an end, a large number of city denizens head towards Indore's heartthrob Sarafa Bazar where they spend the last hours of the day enjoying and relaxing. The name Sarafa Bazar must have given you some idea about the nature of the market. As the sun rests its rays and the moon comes up, the market comes to life, and the people can be seen gathering all around the shops enjoying every moment of it. At around 9 p.m., the excitement of the Sarafa Bazar starts to peak. As the clock ticks away, the influx of people increases, and the market livens up.

This charisma of Sarafa Bazar is the identity of Indore. There must be only a handful of cities in India where a market like this comes to life after sunset. For years, the Sarafa Bazar has been witnessing blissful jamborees. Just imagine: Every night, there is a gathering of people not in hundreds but in thousands in this market. As a handful of people leave for the day, many more come to take their places around different stalls. Usually, at a given time, there may be more than 2,000 people ready to get a taste of life at Sarafa Bazar.

Normally, when about a hundred people gather at a place, there is bound to be trash around. People eating outdoors tend to throw leftovers on the road. Most people in a crowd don't have any idea about how others will be inconvenienced due to the mess they make. But surprisingly, you will not find any such filth or dirt–not even a piece of paper–on the road. Sarafa Bazar remains spick and span, although it is one of the country's most crowded markets and is visited by thousands daily. People enjoy being there and also ensure that others do not face any hardship.

People chill out but keep their surroundings neat and clean. They have learnt the lesson of discipline in an enjoyable way. It is not that Indore was always so neat and tidy. People of the city have always enjoyed eating and drinking and having fun, but there was no awareness about cleanliness. People used to litter and spoil the beauty and the atmosphere of the market. Four years ago, the people of Indore got wind of the *Swachh Bharat Abhiyan* of the Government of India.

The district administration and Indore Municipal Corporation decided that Indore, which was number one in every aspect, must also excel in cleanliness. The goal of transforming a traditional city was a challenge. The administration's initiative gradually started to pay off, and Indore became the winner not once but five times in a row.

This success was due to the administration's efforts and the love of the Indoris towards their city.

When one reaches the Sarafa Bazaar at night, the joyful atmosphere readily brings a smile on one's face. Childhood memories get refreshed. Roadside shops are open, while the regular market is closed. Galleries and lanes are empty, and roadside sellers stand in a disciplined manner on both sides of the road. There is a large number of shops offering a variety of sweets, *namkeen, kachori, golgappas* and new age pizzas and burgers to lure visitors. One can also find shops selling different varieties of *paan* to arouse taste buds. There are no less than ten people in front of a shop at any given time.

There are three to five people managing each shop. At least, one of them there manages the waste. If someone accidentally dumps the garbage, rather than arguing with him, the shopkeeper politely conveys to him to dump the garbage in the garbage box and help in keeping the city clean.

The person littering on the road feels embarrassed. Henceforth, he ensures his family also deposits the garbage in the bin and not on the roadside.

A 60-year-old Gajbhan Gurjar had set up his *golgappa* shop in Sarafa. It has been a while since he set up a shop there. Seeing the welcome changes in the Sarafa in the last few years, his face glows with contentment and working there is now a new experience for him. He says that there was a time when the customers used to throw garbage wherever they wished after eating. They were also careless. In other words, cleanliness was not a part of people's lives, but one now feels one has lived forty years of life in the last five years. Now people are conscious about cleanliness. People are also informed about the harmful effects of littering. They now dump garbage in the garbage box instead of littering their surroundings. It has become a habit to convince each other not to dump garbage anywhere but in the box. We feel proud when people say that they can learn about cleanliness from the people of Indore.

28-year-old Mahesh Nandlal is relieved that his own Indore is clean and is number one in the country. He wants Indore to continue to be the messenger of cleanliness even after this campaign ends. Mahesh says that before the cleanliness drive was launched, they used to dump garbage wherever they wished. Before the cleanliness drive, all kinds of waste, dry or wet, could be found in the same garbage bin. But today, dry garbage and wet garbage are put in different bins. This also helps the sanitation workers to manage the garbage in a better way.

While agreeing with Mahesh Nandlal, Ganesh Pal says that the local administration has put in place a system ensuring that cleaning is done from morning till late night. When the administration has taken such a good initiative, we should also cooperate. The dry and wet garbage bins are kept separately, and when the municipal corporation employees come, they put the dry and wet waste in the different chambers in their vehicles. This reduces their hard work and also saves time which enables them to undertake more cleaning work.

Shrish and Sunita, a young couple visited Sarafa almost every day to have fun. Shrish has his own business, and

Sunita is a housewife. They say that although earlier they enjoyed coming to Sarafa, now there is greater enjoyment and fun. The whole market looks very tidy that they do not feel that they are roaming in the same Sarafa Bazar of Indore, where piles of waste and garbage would be a common sight earlier. They thank the Municipal Corporation for this initiative as the sanitation arrangements earlier were inadequate. They also offered their helping hand in cooperating wholeheartedly with the authorities in keeping the city clean. Our city and the residents enjoy a separate identity, and it is so heartening to see our city at the top place.

When Vinod Bhai, who runs a *jalebi* shop, was asked to pack the savouries in a polythene bag, he refused. On the contrary, he queried if the person was coming to Indore for the first time. He informed him that they had almost stopped using polythene. The bag bank is operational. They deliver goods in paper bags since polythene spoiled the appearance of the city.

The fun-filled evening of Sarafa has a lot to offer: One can see some interesting games going on at one place, and youngsters engaged in some activities somewhere else. In this market of fun and excitement, uncleanliness has become a thing of the past. If you mess up or dump garbage, you can hear the voice of an adult or a child reminding you that this is Indore... None of the visitors, customers, shopkeepers or sanitation workers will let you make the city dirty. They will explain to you that it is our own Indore.

You can see how sensitive an average Indori is towards his city in Sarafa and vibrant Rajwada. A large number of people visit the historic Rajwada throughout the day. Rajwada being a large commercial area, it is difficult to estimate the number of commuters. But the cleanliness of the place sends the message that even in such a crowded area, there is no place for dirt, and Indore has to be clean. People visiting Indore for their work have also got the message that they too have to dump garbage in the allocated bins.

While strolling in Rajwada, if you carelessly or intentionally dump waste, you can hear a voice from behind asking you to put it in the trash box. You cannot escape and run away after throwing the garbage. People will run after you. Nobody will quarrel with you. But they will convince you in such a way that you will think twice before littering in future.

Rajwada is a big market of Indore. Along with other trade and business, one can enjoy the best food here. Usually, such shops and markets generate a lot of garbage and people tend to be careless in maintaining cleanliness but here too one will not find dirt anywhere. There is a garbage box in front of every shop with a written request to put the leftovers only in the trash box after eating. Shopkeepers and vendors solicited customers' cooperation in making Indore clean. One can find beautiful and heart-touching slogans written in Hindi and Malwi seeking the help and support of the people in ensuring cleanliness. Cleanliness is also being taken care of in local transport.

Another distinct attraction of Indore is Chhappan Dukan. There is no need to tell you about Chhappan Dukan if you are from Indore, but you should definitely visit this place if you are from outside Indore. One can eat to one's heart's content. It is a must-visit place for all foodies. Everything from sweets, snacks or *namkeen*, is served here. The Chhappan Dukan means the paradise of taste. It is a great place to relish all street food, *namkeens* and other items. This street is renowned for yummy and cheap snacks and sweets of Indore, including *lassi* and *shikanji* or *raj kachori, golgappe, chaat-pakodi* and Chinese food. One can comfortably sit in front of the shops and relax and click a selfie. Normally, one can hope to find garbage dumped here and there at such a place, but it is not so. There is cleanliness all around.

From the shopkeeper to the customer, everyone is conscious that garbage must be put into the bins. They cooperate with each other wholeheartedly in keeping Indore clean. Chhappan Dukan is similar to Chowpatty of Mumbai. People come here with their families; it is a place of special attraction for the students who come to Indore for studies and those who work here and have made this city their workplace. Chhappan Dukan is everyone's favourite. Although there are so many food delicacies for food lovers, the one thing that no one forgets is to keep the place spotless and sparkling. Indore is setting an example in cleanliness. No one litters here because it is Indore, the cleanest city in the country.

□

13

Cleanest City Tag gives Wings to the Business of Cleaning Industries

Indore was declared as the cleanest city for the first time in 2017 in the nationwide *Swachh Survekshan* 2017, and in the years that followed, that enhanced the mood of the Indoris, and the appearance of the homes and markets changed rapidly.

Before the launch of the *Swachhh Bharat* Mission - Urban, the people were accustomed to seeing rotting heaps of garbage on the roadside and filth lying everywhere, but today, they understand the difference between a clean and dirty city and how it affects their life and health. They do not remain indifferent to unhygienic surroundings. On the other hand, they leave no stone unturned in keeping their surroundings clean, and one can notice a distinct change in the lifestyle of the Indoris. This change was noticed not only in the domestic households but also in offices and markets and the demand for cleaning products used for cleaning the houses, the offices/shops etc. has increased substantially.

Earlier, similar to other cities, the Indoris also did not know the difference between wet and dry garbage, but now they know how to manage waste segregation successfully. For this, different dustbins are being kept in almost every house to collect wet and dry wastes separately. People follow the guidelines regarding the segregation of wastes and cooperate with the sanitation workers of the Municipal Corporation. Due to everyone's efforts, Indore has emerged as the cleanest city.

Indore retained the top place in the cleanliness drive for the fifth consecutive time. Due to this, the industries manufacturing or dealing with cleaning, hygiene and sanitation equipment and items are also continuously expanding their business. Most sanitation equipment is made of plastic. The consumption of plastic in the country is constantly increasing, but the pace is much higher in Indore. Ever since Indore emerged number one in cleanliness, the demand for plastic dustbins, wipers, hand gloves and other cleaning equipment and chemicals has increased substantially. Today, dustbins are available in almost every household. People who did not have dustbins earlier have started keeping at least two dustbins in their homes. This industry has gained momentum due to the inclination of the people towards cleanliness.

Government Initiative

The work of setting up the first plastic lab has begun in Indore. After the establishment of this lab, not only will the industries expand, but the job opportunities for the unemployed youths will also increase. The government is putting up the first plastic lab of the state in the Polo ground Industrial Area of Indore. This is because the rate of growth of the plastic industry in the whole country is 18.5 per cent, whereas, in Indore, this industry is growing at the rate of 28 per cent. Every type of dustbin, big and small, is produced in industries set up in the city. Since 2016, the sale of plastic dustbins and similar items has been steadily increasing. With the increase in materials used for making dustbins and other sanitation items, employment possibilities have got a boost. The plastics industry in Indore is developing rapidly. The youths of Indore and nearby areas are getting jobs here, thanks to these industries.

City can Emerge as Plastic Hub

Pravin Agarwal, national president of India Plastapack Forum, says that the *Swachh Bharat* Mission of the Government of India has not only changed the image and picture of Indore but the entire country, When Indore came first in the campaign, the demand for dustbins and other items used for disposal started increasing. Agarwal says there is a very good potential for the growth of the plastic industry in Indore. He hopes that due to the change in the lifestyle of the people due to the *Swachh Bharat Abhiyan*, the city of Indore will emerge as a plastic hub in the coming years due to its strategic location. More than 250 manufacturers from Indore are associated with the India Plastapack Forum. If the industries expand, the chances of employment for the youth will increase. We hope that the times to come will bring about a better future, Agarwal said.

D.S. Mandloi, director of MSME Development Centre, Indore, said that permission to develop CFC (Common Facility Centre) for plastic manufacturers in Indore is expected to be received soon. The reason for this is that there is a potential for the plastics industry here to grow at a very fast pace. About a year ago, the MSME Development Institute, Indore, received in-principle approval for setting up CFC in plastic cluster to develop the plastics manufacturing industry better in Indore and Ujjain. More than 100 plastic traders in Indore have also requested for a place to set up the industry. According to the data received from the Department of Industries, in 2016, the annual sale of plastic goods and dustbin etc., was around Rs. 200 crores in Indore, while in 2020, this figure increased to around Rs.300 crores. The consumption and turnover of plastic goods are constantly increasing in many areas of the city.

Dustbins of every size are being made here, the cost of which range from Rs. 60 to Rs. 2,250. This includes dustbins used by domestic households and large dustbins kept by the Municipal Corporation in parks, gardens, and roadsides. Apart from this, business ventures of cleaning materials such as wipers, brushes, brooms and phenyl etc., is also rapidly growing. Usually, phenyl is used in the houses of Indore. Now, its demand has increased manifold because the outlook of people towards cleanliness has changed. The business of cleaning chemicals etc. is also constantly increasing. The chemical business is expected to grow further in the times to come. Dustbin, broom and other equipment made of plastic are being manufactured on a large scale in the industrial areas of Indore.

Ramesh Gidwani, a businessman, shares his experience and says that given the spirit of cleanliness in the city, there is ample scope for the growth of the plastic and chemical industry in the coming years. Our turnover from the business was Rs. 200 crores in 2016; now, it has increased to around Rs. 300 crores. This figure also is likely to be surpassed soon because plastic is also being recycled here. The recycling process became easy after the Municipal Corporation installed a plastic separating machine in the trenching ground. People associated with this business believe that their business has steadily grown due to the cleanliness drive.

One of the reasons behind this is that small villages, towns and cities around the city that run their business from Indore are also now buying more plastic goods because there is a growing awareness about cleanliness. In Indore, dustbins of circular, rectangular shapes, open and closed ranging from 10 litres to 200-litre capacity and in some places up to 2,000 litres capacity are being used.

They are also being replaced with time; hence the industry is now constantly growing.

Thousands of Jobs...

Presently, there are about 300 factories making plastic in the city of Indore. These factories employ 5-10,000 people. There are around 200 wholesalers and more than 8,00,000 retail traders. About a quarter of the people are permanently employed. Harish Motwani, president of Indore Plastic Manufacturers Association says that people engaged in other businesses are also attracted towards this business due to increase in sales of plastic products. The plastics industry is gaining momentum due to the rising demand due to the efforts of the public in making Indore dirt and pollution-free.

Along with the production of plastic, the wholesale and open trade in the market has also increased manifolds. Apart from the hot market of Indore, the demand for these items is increasing in neighbouring places as well. In five years, all the government schemes put together have not generated as many employment opportunities as the plastic industry has done in the recent years.

Business Projected to Double

Despite reduction in the use of plastics in many states and increasing awareness among people about the damage it causes to the environment, the plastics industry is projected to double its business to Rs. 5 lakh crores by 2025. According to the All-India Plastics Manufacturers Association (AIPMA), the size of the plastics industry at present is Rs. 2.25 lakh crores. This industry employs 45 lakh people. Indore accounts for eight per cent of the country's total business. With proper government support, the turnover of the plastics industry can double to Rs. 5 lakh crores in the next five years. Since plastic products do not last for a long time, the demand continues to rise. Recycling of used plastics has made the way for the industry to reuse them.

After joining the *Swachh Bharat Abhiyan*, awareness has increased among the residents of Indore. After winning the title of *Swachh* Indore, plastic is largely being used, but care is also to prevent throwing plastic items in open areas after use. The citizens of Indore are also trying to save the environment from any harm. As the use of plastic products is increasing, there is also a need to recycle them. The Municipal Corporation is paying due attention to this. Plastic is not being used indiscriminately; on the other hand, the focus is on using it judiciously and recycling it as much as possible to lessen the undue burden on the city and ensure that the environment remains safe.

□

14
Eco-Friendly Pots

The Indore Municipal Corporation (IMC) and Basix Municipal Waste Ventures Limited (BMWV) came up with an innovative idea of making cow dung pots for nurseries to grow saplings. This innovation aims to reduce the use of plastic bags as plants from most nurseries sell the little saplings in plastic bags. Once the plants are transferred to mud or cement pots, the plastic bags are discarded. They either end up in landfills or are burnt – causing pollution and harming the environment. Even worse, the animals end up eating them and consequently die from stomach ailments.

Cow dung or cow manure has been used for ages in Indian agriculture to nourish the soil and help plant growth. Cow dung is enriched with high levels of minerals and nutrients and is one of the best natural fertilisers for gardening. Keeping all these qualities of cow dung in mind, the Municipal Corporation decided to manufacture cow dung pots for which cow dung pot making machine was installed at Regional Park.

Now, pots are being made involving just a few steps by the BMWV team members at Regional Park. The first step involves bringing fresh cow dung from the gaushala of the IMC to the Regional Park. Then one week old cow dung is added to that fresh dung. After this, the cow dung is filtered to remove impurities like stones. After filtering, it is repeatedly mixed for 10-15 minutes with a powder in the mixing machine with some water (to increase the strength of the pot), and then this mixture is transported to the mould of the pot making machine. Compressing with manual effort is the next step. Then the compressed pot is removed from the machine, and finally, the pot is dried for 24 hours.

The pots are sturdy, made from pure cow dung and resistant to pests. It is easy to manufacture and is an environmentally friendly product.

About 25,000 pots have been made out of which 15,000

pots have been given to the IMC for gardening.

Impacts:

Cow dung pots will reduce the use of plastic bags, which causes pollution and sickness in animals.

Cow dung manure is enriched with high levels of minerals and nutrients and is one of the best natural fertilisers for gardening.

Nursery owners will also get benefit from these cow dung pots, and their source of income will also increase.

□

15

Garden Waste Management

Every year, the Indore Municipal Corporation undertakes measures to enhance and further streamline the solid waste management system that is in place in the city. Consequently, in 2020, the IMC decided to chalk out a unique strategy to channelise the bulk garden and horticulture waste generated in the city.

Bulk garden and horticultural waste refer to the bulk waste from parks, gardens, traffic islands, road medians etc. including grass and wood clippings, weeds, woody 'brown' carbon-rich material such as pruning, branches, twigs, wood chipping, straw or dead leaves and tree trimmings, which cannot be accommodated in the daily collection system for bio-degradable waste.

The IMC has 569 gardens, in which it has constructed 366 composting pits. A select few gardens had space constraints and were therefore clubbed together with the nearest garden with enough space to treat their landscape waste. The action plan devised for the bulk garden and horticultural waste ensures that the entire landscape and garden waste generated from these 569 gardens is treated and converted into compost in these 366 composting pits.

Through diligent monitoring and exhaustive IEC drives for successful implementation, the IMC has ensured that all residents in the city practice source segregation of waste into 6 different categories. It has trained the *safai mitras* and other concerned workers to keep the bulk garden and horticultural waste unmixed, i.e. separated from regular waste, especially other wet waste and compost it on site. In lieu thereof, it has also encouraged residents to store the garden and horticulture waste, including tree and plant trimmings, from their private gardens separately. The residents have been advised to convert the garden cuttings from their homes into compost or hand it over to the dedicated IMC vehicles assigned for this purpose.

For the collection and transportation of bulk garden and horticultural waste, the IMC has 12 dedicated trucks and 85 open tippers of 5 cum capacity, allocated in each of the 85 wards to collect waste green and horticulture waste.

In October 2020, the IMC installed two Drum Composter of 10 TPD each at Meghdoot garden and near Sirpur transfer station to process the garden waste, including the tree cuttings from roadside plantation within the city, tree cuttings and landscape waste from households and also green waste and fallen leaves on the roads collected from sweeping of roads.

The garden waste management plan ensures that the IMC collects and processes 100% of the garden and horticultural waste generated in the city. The fact that it reuses the compost in the same gardens and parks adds to both the uniqueness and circularity of the overall system.

□

16

Wet Waste Processing Facilities

The Indore Municipal Corporation has established centralised and decentralised processing plants for wet waste in the city. The processing facilities together have adequate capacity to ensure that 100% of the wet waste generated in the city is processed so that no wet waste is left unprocessed on any day.

Biomethanation (Bio-CNG) Plants

The Indore Municipal Corporation (IMC) had previously undertaken a unique Waste to Energy conversion initiative to discourage the practice of using petroleum in public transport and curb air pollution. The fact that the plants in the country generated 95% pure methane (later converted into CNG) added twice as much to its uniqueness. It had tied up with Mahindra Waste to Energy Solutions Ltd. to establish the 15 TPD capacity plant at Kabit Khedi at a cost recovery period of five years besides social, environmental and economic benefits.

The plant undergoes an anaerobic digestion process,

which takes place in a closed airtight digester where organic raw materials such as manure, food waste, sewage sludge and organic industrial waste are converted into biogas and digestate end products. The produced biogas is a mixture of 50 (70% methane) and 30 (50% carbon dioxide) and smaller amounts of water vapour, hydrogen sulphide and other minor components and trace elements. The result is a gas comprising mainly of methane, which increases its energy content.

The clean, upgraded biogas can be used as fuel for cars, buses and trucks. With the success of both the plants, IMC has taken a step forward and proposed a 500 TPD biomethanation plant to be set up at Devguradiya disposal site with IL&FS Environmental Infrastructure & Services Limited. Under the PPP model, the company shall incur 100% capital investment with a concession of 20 years for the said project. It is expected that within a span of one year, over 100 buses will operate on Bio-CNG.

Waste to Compost Plant

The Centralised Organic Waste Processing Unit is the waste-to-compost plant situated at the disposal site at Devguradiya. The plant was commissioned in 2009 and had an installed capacity to process 600 MT of wet MSW.

The compost plant is working to its capacity of 600 MT of wet waste per day. Weigh Bridge facility is established at the central processing plant. This is the first point of interaction for all the vehicles coming in at the plant. This is a computerised facility where the weight of all the wet waste collected by the door-to-door collection and the bulk collection system is brought to be weighed before it can move to the processing plant.

Garden Waste Management

In order to channelise wet waste management in the city, the IMC has devised a garden waste management plan. Bulk garden and horticultural waste refer to bulk waste from parks, gardens, traffic islands, road medians etc. including grass and wood clippings, weeds, woody 'brown' carbon-rich material such as pruning, branches, twigs, wood chipping, straw or dead leaves and tree trimmings, which cannot be accommodated in the daily collection system for bio-degradable waste.

The total capacity for wet waste processing as devised in the garden waste management plan is 59 TPD. Moreover, as part of garden waste management, the IMC has 12 dedicated trucks for collecting and transporting garden waste. Additionally, it has 85 open Tippers of 5 cum capacity that have been allocated to each of the 85 wards in the city.

Energy Bins

The IMC has installed an Energy Bin, which runs on 12KW electricity to process wet waste. The stainless-steel drum mixes wet waste with wastewater and generates slurry that produces biogas transferred in balloons encased in metal boxes. The collected gas is used for filling cylinders under pressure or for running generators to produce electricity. The entire unit is firmly enclosed in a metal body, leaving no scope for any harmful gases or stench to leak out.

Mobile Composting Units

The IMC has hired Swaaha Resource Management Private Limited for the use of mobile composting units. The mobile vans process up to 250 kgs of waste per hour, consuming only 1 unit of electricity for every 100 kg of waste. The IMC uses the mobile vans of Swaaha to cater to wet waste generated from multi-storied apartments and RWAs. Additionally, the IMC also uses mobile vans for special zero-waste events to generate vast amounts of waste.

Home Composting

At present, over 50,000 households' practice on site composting in the city of Indore. The IMC has empanelled four Non-Governmental organisations (NGOs) that support its various activities for socio-behavioural cultural change and implementation of various innovative practices. Thus, the NGOs and IMC regularly conduct drives to encourage more residents to practice on site composting. To avail technical assistance or any help for home composting, the residents have two options, i.e. they can either seek help from the NGOs during the daily morning door to door collection of waste wherein the volunteers regularly visit houses to ensure that source segregation is being practised correctly. Additionally, the residents can also reach out through the Indore 311 App.

Bulk Waste Generators and Residential Welfare Associations

For Bulk Waste Generators and Residential Welfare Associations, the IMC primarily encourages in-situ composting. 287 such units practice it via various means such as on-site waste composters, community pit composting, etc. The IMC has a dedicated vehicle for collecting and transporting wet waste for the remaining that cannot do so.

The IMC is in the process of establishing a 550 TPD capacity biomethanation plant with NTPC, which will treat inert waste emerging from both wet and dry waste. This plant will help the IMC to establish itself as the first one million-plus population zero landfill city.

□

17

Introducing the Concept of Zero Waste to the City of Indore

Zero Waste Temples

In 2015, the IMC, for the first time, introduced the concept of zero waste through its unique initiative of Zero Waste Temple. Khajrana Ganesh Temple is one of the most important temples in the city that generated over 200-300 kgs of floral waste daily. Thus, under the PPP model, the IMC appointed an agency that would carry out floral waste management in the city. For this purpose, 3-5 feet rooms were given to the agency. The initiative was formally launched on 19th September 2015. With the active cooperation of shopkeepers and devotees, the temple was able to produce 50-60 kgs of organic compost. Post the success of the Khajrana Temple, other important temples in the city such as Bijasan Temple, Sai Temple, Shani Temple, Balaji Temple, Vaishnav Temple, etc., also began to implement similar models.

Zero Waste Events

Every year, the Dawoodi Bohra community from across the world meets for a 10-day long event. In 2018, the event was held in Indore between 12th to 22nd September and was particularly special as it was the first time when the 53rd Dai-al-Mutlaq, head of the Bohra community, His Holiness Syedna Mufaddal Saifuddin, conducted the Ashara sermons in Indore. Over 15 lakh Dawoodi Bohras from different countries joined the sermons.

It was expected that vast quantities of both dry and wet waste would be generated at the event. However, the highly motivated Bohra community and the event organisers, i.e., the Burhani Foundation, decided to convert the event into a zero-waste event. A process in partnership with the IMC and its stakeholders was designed that ensured no 'waste' was to be generated at the event. The measures undertaken to achieve the goal included the complete ban of single-use plastic, source segregation of the waste, on-site recycling of the dry waste, etc. Furthermore, approximately 250 MT of wet waste was converted into compost by the Mobile Compost Unit from Swaaha. As a symbolic gesture, the religious head himself handed over the compost to some of the attendees. The remaining compost was given to the farmers for use in agriculture.

Thereafter, between 7th-10th October 2019, the highly active Maharashtrian community in Indore organised Jathra, a Maharashtrian food festival. The three-day long festival had over 5 to 6 lakh people attending it. The festival in 2019 was special, for it was the first time the festival was conducted by adopting the 3R Principle. The festival had 500 stalls of food, artisan and handicraft products.

In order to successfully implement the action plan, 20 counters were set up, with each counter being handled by four volunteers. Half the volunteers were engaged in the process of segregation of wet waste, and the other half were engaged in transporting the waste to the designated vehicles. The event generated over 6,678 kgs of MSW, and over 50% of it was converted to compost. The vendors, through shared consensus, made use of only biodegradable products, while plastic, cling foils, aluminium etc. were strictly prohibited. Infrastructural facilities such as counters for waste collection through wet and dry waste bins enabled efficient collection, sorting and disposal of waste. Through careful planning, the food festival presented the usage of 7,000 square feet of flex, 1,700 square feet of aluminium foil, 12,000 plastic glass, 5,000 plastic bowls, 2,00,000 plastic spoons, 2,25,000 polythene bags, 200 square feet of plastic wraps and 10,000 pet bottles. Besides, 2,220 kg of organic compost was generated.

Between 14th and 16th November, 2019, the IMC and the Madhya Pradesh Cricket Board joined hands to host the India v/s Bangladesh Test Match as a zero-waste event. For the event, special IEC materials with positive messages were displayed in the form of stickers, banners and hoardings, and extensive digital media coverage was initiated to promote cleanliness, ban on single-use plastic and disposables within the stadium. During the event, over 4,261 kgs of segregated waste were generated and collected. The dry waste was sent directly to the authorised recyclers, and the wet waste was converted into compost through on site processing with the help of Swaaha.

When introduced to the idea of zero waste, the mobilised residents of Indore began to organise citizen-led zero-waste events such as weddings, parties etc. The residents reached out to the NGOs or the IMC for technical assistance and support i needed in organising the events.

Zero Waste Premises

In 2019, for the first time, the Collector's Office in Indore was declared a Zero Waste Premise. The entire dry waste generated was recycled and processed in a mini-Material Recovery Centre within the office itself. The wet waste from the mess was processed and converted into compost in the garden within the premises. Any inert waste generated was the only waste that was handed over to the IMC. For its successful implementation, training workshops were conducted for source segregation of waste for the staff and the workers handling the waste, ban on single-use plastic bags and all disposable items such as thermacol etc., and placement of twin bins in the halls of all the offices halls etc.

Zero Waste Societies

Not to be left behind, the residents of select societies began to express their desire to establish their societies as zero waste societies. Such societies include Parmanu Nagar, RRCAT, New York City, Victory Urban etc. With technical support from NGO partners in their respective zones, these societies ensured that at least the dry and wet waste generated was recycled and processed within the society's premises only. Only certain waste that needed centralised city level processing facilities, such as construction and demolition waste, domestic hazardous waste etc., were handed over to the IMC.

The Initiative

With the residents well acquainted with the idea of zero waste, especially the environmental benefits associated with it, it was but natural that the seed of zero waste wards began to germinate in the minds of the residents.

Consequently, the IMC, for the first time in August 2020, saw residents from two wards come forward and express their desire to establish their wards as zero waste wards. The change makers of both the wards reached out to the NGOs assigned to their wards for door-to-door collection and IEC activities for technical assistance, which the latter enthusiastically agreed to provide. Through word of mouth, the activities of both the wards began to spread like wildfire to other wards in the city.

Very soon, in the following months, the residents of three other wards came forward and accepted the challenge of establishing their wards as zero waste wards as well. The most unique and novel feature about the entire conversation about zero waste wards was that it was completely a citizen level initiative, wherein the residents themselves came forward and committed to not just achieving their goal but also ensuring that the rest of the residents would follow suit in realising their vision.

Unsurprisingly, the torch bearers of the zero-waste ward in Ward No 73 were the Bohra community living in the ward. Committed to the cause since 2018, during the Ashara Mubarak, the community members initiated various measures to realise the promises made for adopting waste reduction measures and zero-waste lifestyles.

The group reached out to the NGO working in the ward, i.e. Basix Municipal Ventures Private Limited, to provide technical assistance to accomplish the goal. Thereafter, training workshops and meetings were conducted to discuss the action plan and strategising on the measures that had to be undertaken. What was particularly challenging for the ward was that it was the first ward in the city to face such a daunting yet exciting challenge. Hence, there was no reference or precedent case study that they could follow.

Around the same time as Ward 73, Ward 47 also came forward with the determination to establish their ward as a zero-waste ward. The residents of Ward 47 were sensitised to the zero-waste idea. Through community engagement, the residents were habituated to witness, participate and initiate various waste reduction measures in their lives, both at the individual and community levels. Some of the measures included developing a 4R garden with over 3200 pet bottles, 5000 bottle caps and 8 tons of municipal solid waste collected from the ward.

The leaders of Ward 47 were residents from Regal Colony, Agra Vihar Colony, Joy Builder's Colony, Scheme 91, 56 Dukaan and Racecourse Road. Taking a cue from Ward 73, the residents of Ward 47 also reached out to Human Matrix Solutions, an NGO for technical support.

The momentum for the zero-waste ward in Ward 47 also picked up from the fact that colonies in the ward started establishing themselves as zero waste colonies or societies. One such colony was the Joy Builder's colony, where the entire colony practised home composting. Moreover, the decentralised MRF was established at the ward, accompanied by the slow phasing out of municipal services and rolling out of self-services. Thus, the residents were acquainted firsthand with the benefits of decentralised modes of processing.

Meetings and training sessions were conducted with the members initially, and then slowly, other residents of the colony started joining as well. Through persuasion and sheer trust in the larger cause, the residents joined hands with the NGO and conducted a door-to-door campaign to motivate all the residents to participate. The residents were persuaded to practice home composting, and those who were unable to do so due to lack of space were encouraged to hand over their wet waste for community composting or mobile composting.

Looking at the success of both the wards, residents from Ward 4, 32 and 66 also decided to participate. In Ward 32, the ward had been divided into clusters to conduct focused interventions for home composting, source segregation etc. The heads of the cluster committees decided in their weekly meetings that they would transform their ward as a zero-waste ward. The cluster committee heads pledged that they would conduct door-to-door campaigns in their respective clusters and ensure that all households would practice home composting. Moreover, the cluster committee heads also educated the residents on six types of categorisation: decentralised dry waste collection, discouraging using single-use disposable items in everyday lives etc.

Elsewhere, Ward 4 has its own unique story as in this ward, for the first time, a women's only group came forward for the cause of zero waste. The highly active group was already a driving force in successfully reaching out and persuading households in the wards to practice home composting. The Women and the Divine, an NGO for technical support, helped with the composting activities already underway to promote dry waste segregation and adopt 3R practices in their everyday lives.

The Implementation Plan

With the technical assistance from the NGOs, the city's residents, associations, communities and change makers came forward to accomplish the dream of zero waste wards. Given the positive response to the exhaustive city level practices introduced by the IMC, such as six types of source segregation, sensitisation towards MSW, the torch bearers of respective wards were able to motivate and mobilise the remaining residents living in the wards.

Wet Waste

Wet waste refers to biodegradable waste that includes all organic materials which micro-organisms can degrade into simpler stable compounds. In the identified zero waste wards, it was decided to maximise on-site composting so that there was no requirement for the assistance of a centralised wet waste processing facility.

Home Composting: With assistance from the NGOs, the residents, especially those living in independent apartments and houses were given composting units to facilitate home composting. These composting units were primarily of two types- terracotta and green bins. The composting units were given to the residents at a 50% rebate, with the other 50% paid by the CSR partners. Those who had their private gardens also had the added option of composting their wet waste through pits.

For handholding and technical assistance, the residents were provided with a helpline number to seek any assistance needed for composting. Additionally, the residents could also reach out to the NGOs or the IMC through Indore 311 App. Once the compost was ready, the residents were encouraged to reuse the compost in their own gardens or hand it over to the NGOs for reuse in the nearby parks and gardens.

Community Composting: The wards also have several multi-storied apartments and slum areas, where lack of space prevents residents from practising home composting. In such instances, the residents are advised to practice community composting instead, wherein common pits are made in the gardens (within the ward boundary) to process their organic waste and convert it into compost. At present, community composting is practised only in ward number 47, with 1892 households attached to it.

Mobile Composting Units: There is a third mode for onsite processing of organic waste for residents who cannot practice home composting, which is mobile composting units, wherein specially designed vehicles by Swaaha Resource Management Private Limited collect and convert the organic waste into compost. The users of this service pay user charges ranging from Rs. 750-2,500, depending on the locality, amount of waste etc.

Furthermore, it is to be noted that the guidelines for processing MSW, all BWGs generating waste over 50 kgs of MSW per day, practice on site composting of their organic waste. The semi-BWGs, generating waste between 10-50 kgs of MSW, practice on site composting either through the help of community composting or through mobile composting units.

In order to ensure the recycling of resources, the compost generated in the 5 wards is either used by the residents themselves in their own gardens or handed over to the NGOs for use in the parks and gardens in the wards.

Dry Waste

As per the SWM Rules 2016, dry waste refers to waste other than bio-degradable and inert street sweeping and includes recyclables and non-recyclable waste, combustible waste, sanitary napkins and diapers, etc.

In the implementation plan developed for the zero waste wards, dry waste includes two further categorisations, i.e., plastic waste and non-plastic waste. The segregated dry waste of both categories is collected and transported to the four Decentralised Material Recovery Facilities (MRF) established in four out of the four wards (the fifth ward shares an MRF as it is the adjacent ward). At the MRFs, the collected waste is segregated further into more than eight categories. Thereafter the segregated waste is reused, recycled, up cycled or sent to authorised recyclers for further processing and reuse.

Moreover, in the five zero-waste wards, the decentralised dry waste collection also occurs, wherein residents have been given sacks that can store up to approximately 10 kgs of waste. The residents segregate and store valuable dry waste in these sacks, which the NGOs collect every 15 or 30 days. The dry waste is sold at Rs. 2.50 per kilogram. The direct impact of this initiative is that it significantly improves the quality of recyclables as well as incentives received from the segregation of waste.

The four decentralised MRFs in the zero waste wards have the requisite operational capacity to process the dry waste generated in the wards.

Electronic Waste, Domestic Hazardous Waste and Sanitary Waste

The SWM Rules 2016 refers to domestic hazardous waste as waste including discarded paint drums, pesticide cans, CFL bulbs, tube lights, expired medicines, broken mercury thermometers, used batteries, used needles and syringes and contaminated gauge, etc., generated at the household level, and sanitary waste as waste comprising of used diapers, sanitary towels or napkins, tampons, condoms, incontinence sheets and any other similar waste. Likewise, the E-Waste (Management) Rules 2016 refers to e-waste as waste consisting of electrical and electronic equipment, whole or in part discarded as waste by the consumer or bulk consumer, as well as rejects from manufacturing, refurbishment and repair processes.

As the handling of these three types of waste is to be done with utmost precaution and its scientific processing can only be done at the city level, the IMC had deployed one dedicated vehicle to collect and transport the three types of waste to their assigned processing facilities.

Waste Generated from Street Sweeping

In order to optimise the processing of MSW, segregation of road sweeping waste into three categories, i.e., dry, wet and inert, was introduced. The streets have three sacks placed in designated corners, wherein the *safaimitras* store the segregated waste. The vehicle route charts have been carefully designed to collect the segregated sweeping waste and transport it safely, in a segregated manner, to the respectively processing facilities. Thus, the wet is transferred to the nearest parks and gardens for conversion into compost, whereas the dry and inert waste is taken to the decentralised MRF. The dry waste is further segregated and recycled, and inert waste is sent to the sanitary landfill and the other designated landfill every week.

Garden Waste Management

Bulk garden and horticultural waste refer to the bulk waste from parks, gardens, traffic islands, road medians etc. including grass & wood clippings, weeds, woody 'brown' carbon-rich material such as pruning, branches, twigs, wood chipping, straw or dead leaves and tree trimmings, which cannot be accommodated in the daily collection system for bio-degradable waste.

Through a one-of-its-kind initiative, the IMC has developed a unique action plan to process the bulk garden and horticulture waste generated in over 569 gardens in the city. This has been replicated in the zero waste wards and all the organic waste generated in the parks and garden.

Impact

Environmental Impact

Reduction in Waste

The first and foremost impact of the zero waste wards has been a reduction in waste generation. A citizen level movement, the residents of the wards, are essentially individuals who are highly sensitised to the issues on waste generation and the number of resources and energy required to process or dispose of it. As a result, they have undertaken and motivated others living in their neighbourhood to adopt various measures to reduce the amount of waste generated. This includes positive practices such as avoiding the usage of single-use plastics and maximising the use of alternatives such as *thailas* from recycled clothes.

Supporting and practising the IMC campaign of Bring Your Recyclables, thereby significantly reducing the amount of waste generation of plastic disposables, plastic water bottles, etc.

The declaration of all public and commercial areas such as markets, tourist spots, transport hubs, etc., within the ward as plastic and disposable free areas.

Reduction in per capita carbon footprint, which is one of the most critical achievements of the initiative in the long run.

Reduction in Amount of Waste to be Processed

The direct consequence of the reduction in the amount of waste generation is the reduction in the amount of MSW that needs to be processed. The dry waste is 100% recycled in the zero waste wards, and 100% of the wet waste is converted into compost by various modes. Only the categories of waste that require the city level processing facilities such as domestic hazardous waste, sanitary waste, electronic waste and construction and demolition waste are sent outside the ward boundaries. The decentralised modes of processing the wet and dry waste have had advantages like quick disposal of waste, reduction in waste management cost, saving valuable land and better utilisation of human & financial resources.

Decentralised modes of processing of wet and dry waste result in reducing the pressures on the centralised processing facilities of the city.

Reduction in financial expenses incurred on Collection and Transportation Enhanced quality of recyclables due to decentralised processing facilities Reduction in Carbon Footprint & Green House Gas Emissions.

The reduction in the amount of waste generation leads to a corresponding decrease in the overall amount of waste processed. The decentralised modes of processing of dry and wet waste further add to the list of advantages of the initiative by reducing the number of fuels and energy required to collect and transport the waste to the centralised processing facilities.

However, apart from the above-mentioned impact, this unique initiative has a latent yet highly important impact. The self-awareness of the residents towards the waste that they generate has led to a change in the composition of waste generated as well. This has led to a substantial decrease in the amount of inert waste generated in the ward, particularly apparent compared to the inert waste generated in the rest of the city. With the establishment of the zero-waste initiative in the wards, the generation of inert waste in the wards has decreased from 4% to a staggering 1-1.5% only.

Reduction in Rate of Inert Waste Generation from 4% to 1-1.5%

The significant decrease in inert waste generation has led to a decrease in the contribution of inert waste by these wards to the scientific landfill that exists in the city. This leads to a highly coveted reduction in carbon and Green House Gas (GHG) emissions. Moreover, the carbon footprints and GHG emissions caused due to dumping of waste and collection and transportation of MSW are also averted due to zero dump sites and vulnerable garbage points in the ward (and city) and decentralised modes of processing.

Additionally, the organic waste that undergoes on site processing and gets converted to compost also significantly impacts the overall carbon footprints. Based on the standard market practices and UNFCC guidelines, it is assumed that with every single tonne of reduction in wet waste, approximately 300 kgs of methane and GHG liberation is eliminated. Consequently, with every single tonne of organic waste composted, approximately 6,300 kgs of carbon dioxide elimination are averted, or roughly 6 carbon credits can be achieved. These efforts have also enabled IMC to achieve the mandated United Nations Sustainable Development Goals

With every single tonne of organic waste that is composted, approximately 300 kgs of methane and GHG liberation is averted, and roughly 6 carbon credits achieved.

Social Impact

Social Ownership and Accountability

The zero-waste ward initiative is a completely citizen-led initiative, which has primarily emerged from the self-motivation and drive of the residents towards achieving and living in a clean, green and healthy city. A sense of social ownership and accountability has emerged in the city's residents. They feel responsible for their everyday habits and actions, the resultant waste generated, the outcome of waste generated, and the possible recycling, reuse, or reduction.

The social ownership felt by residents has been the propelling force behind the initiative being widely accepted by all the residents of the wards and transforming it from an initiative undertaken by a group of concerned individuals to a Jan Andolan that has cut across different communities and socio-economic classes. It is worth mentioning that despite the given differences in the ward demographics, a common factor in all the five wards has been the role played by women, especially housewives who have made the efforts to make conscious and deliberate lifestyle changes in their homes that have made the initiative successful.

Zero Waste Households and Quality of Lives

Like all other social changes, the novel concept of zero waste must begin at home to succeed at a larger level, i.e., ward, city or national level. In order to achieve the larger goal of the successful establishment of a zero-waste ward, conscious efforts are made at the household level for both waste reduction and processing. Thus, residents have become more aware of their everyday habits and practices and emulate positive practices that lead to the desired reductions.

Over time, with technical support from NGOs, waste segregation has improved considerably. This has enabled two things: 1. The segregated dry waste has improved the quality of recyclables and the corresponding rates when sold for recycling and reuse. 2. The quality of compost from the wet waste generated has improved significantly. This leads to enhanced quality of yields in kitchen gardens, i.e., organic fruits and vegetables devoid of chemicals and pesticides. Thus, over a period, it is expected that the overall health and well-being of the residents will also improve.

Economic Impact

a. Reduction in Collection and Transportation Cost

The decentralised modes of processing and the complete processing of dry and wet waste within the ward have led to a massive decrease in fuel, human resources, and maintenance cost of vehicles earlier associated with the collection and transportation of MSW. At present, only one vehicle of the IMC caters to each of the five wards, and the NGOs operate five vehicles in the ward. It is to be noted that all IMC staff who worked in the identified wards and are no longer needed have been reassigned and given duty elsewhere, so that they do not lose their means of earning their livelihood.

Prior to the establishment of zero waste wards, the IMC operated roughly six vehicles in every ward. The cost of one such vehicle is approximately Rs. 6,50,000. Thus, with six vehicles operating in each of the five wards, the IMC total cost incurred would amount to Rs. 1,95,00,000 only as fixed costs. Additionally, other related expenses like fuel, maintenance, waste collection, and transportation cost have been averted.

Furthermore, in every vehicle, a minimum of two human resources, i.e., a driver and a Safai Mitra, were deployed. If the combined average salary of both is Rs. 12,000, then the IMC saved the cost incurred on 12 human resources in every ward. Thus, the IMC saved Rs. 1,44,000 in every ward and Rs. 7,20,000 combined in all five wards.

With the successful introduction of zero waste wards, the IMC saves over Rs. 22,88,700 every month and Rs. 2,74,64,400 every year.

b. Reduction in Amount of Waste to be Processed in Centralised Facilities

The decentralised processing modes have led to reductions in expenses incurred in operations and maintenance of the centralised processing facilities. The wet waste is 100% processed through different modes of on-site composting, whereas the dry waste is recycled in the decentralised MRFs. Both the decentralised dry waste collection and MRFs have led to an improvement in the quality of the recyclables and an improvement in recycling. The following table elucidates the quantity of waste processed within the wards and thereby reduces total waste sent to the centralised processing facilities.

Livelihood Generation and Self-Employment Opportunities

The zero-waste wards and the establishment of various requisite facilities have led to income-generating opportunities for many, especially the former ragpickers who have been formalised into the system. Thus, at least 1 supervisor, 4 operators, and 10 ragpickers have been given employment opportunities in every MRF.

The decentralised modes of processing have given employment opportunities to at least 15 ragpickers and increased their income from 100-150 per day to Rs. 400-450 per day.

Business Opportunities

The zero-waste wards have opened a new window for business opportunities to various enterprises, startups, etc. For instance, the CSR partners have encouraged the promotion of home composting in the wards, and Swaaha Resource Management Private Limited plays an integral role in enabling the ward to achieve 100% processing of wet waste through its mobile composting vans.

Novelty

The most critical novelty of the initiative is that it is a completely citizen-led innovation, wherein the ULB, i.e., the IMC, has little or no role to play. Rather, the initiative encapsulates the spirit of a Jan Andolan and the power of the people's will. The initiative epitomises the spirit of the people, by the people and of the people.

Moreover, for the first time in the country's history the five wards came together successfully to establish themselves as zero waste wards. Moreover, this was achieved with all the mandated social waste management guidelines applicable and implemented in the city. Through the sheer hard work of residents, NGOs, SHGs, CSOs, etc., the organically developed model showcased a successful model not just for reduction in collection and transportation but also reduction in waste generation. Thus, all residents and commercial, institutional, educational establishments have unitedly and purposefully reduced their waste generation, especially plastic waste generation, by adopting 3R practices such as bringing your own recyclables, disposable free markets, using *jholas* and *bartans* from and *jhola* and *bartan* banks, etc.

Furthermore, the decentralised modes of processing helped generate employment and livelihood opportunities for ragpickers and other people in need. Furthermore, the formalisation helped them acquire a sense of dignity in their work, which was previously missing. The decentralised model of processing and the financial viability of the model enabled the IMC to utilise its resources in other critical developmental activities of the city.

Another attribute that adds to the novelty of this innovation is that the IMC, in order to add value and credibility to the innovation, without any biases, appointed a third-party assessment organisation to assess the claims of the residents of the wards. The Indore School of Social Work was thus appointed by the IMC to carry out the assessment. The Indore School of Social Work carried out the assessment in January 2021, and on 20th January, declared the wards to be zero waste wards.

Scalability

Given the success of the five wards, the IMC seeks to motivate the remaining 80 wards of the city to follow suit and slowly but steadily declare themselves to be zero waste wards. The IMC strives to motivate five wards in the city to transform themselves as zero waste wards every year. This would help establish itself as a zero-waste city, wherein every ward will be a microcosm of the larger sustainable whole, based on decentralised modes of processing. This shall slowly phase out the need for operating centralised processing facilities, at least for dry and wet waste. Moreover, the organically developed model can be replicated and scaled to cities with both higher, lower and equivalent population.

A driving force behind the success of any model or initiative is the financial sustainability of the model. Consequently, the zero-waste model envisaged by the residents and NGOs is based on a self-sustainable financial model, which benefits both the residents and the implementing agency. Thus, on the one hand, the residents avail a 50% rebate in user charges if they are practising on site composting and can sell their recyclables at Rs. 2.50 kg. Likewise, the implementing agency or supporting agency can generate an overall revenue of Rs. 4,18,800 per month. This translates into a monthly profit of over Rs. 1 lakh rupees, given the average expenditure incurred on operations and maintenance to be around Rs. 3 lakhs.

Thus, the models' scalability is proved and shows how it can be scaled up in other wards of the city and other cities of the country.

Way Forward

With this initiative, the IMC hopes that other cities and zones outside cities can follow and replicate the model. Instead of spending resources on facilities, the focus should be on motivating individuals to take the lead and implement such innovative measures.

Moreover, given the annual rise in population and the consequent increase in waste generation, the IMC believes that the decentralised modes of processing will help it meet the foreseeable gap in processing capacities between waste generation and operational capacity of the centralised plants in the future.

□

18

Carbon Credits: Moving Towards a Clean and Green City

The Indore Municipal Corporation (IMC) is the first municipal corporation in the country and Asia that successfully sold carbon credits and generated a significant amount of revenue, i.e., to the tune of Rs. 50 lakhs from it.

Carbon Credits Revenue Carbon credits are certificates issued to entities that reduce their emission of GHG (greenhouse gases), which causes global warming. Carbon credits are measured in units of certified emission reductions (CERs). Each CER is equivalent to one ton of carbon dioxide reduction.

The IMC had successfully registered its project under the VCS mechanism within seven months from the commencement of work, completed the monitoring and verification process based on the operational data of a one-year period, and generated 1.70 lakh Carbon Credits. IMC sold the credits at Rs. 52 lakhs (after paying registration and issuance charges), and the project credit period is for 30 years, i.e., from 2017 to 2047.

The Way Forward

The IMC is applying for other projects that have reduced the carbon level in the environment, including solar projects and conversion of diesel vehicles to CNG and electric vehicles, and efficient disposal of municipal waste. Once these projects are fully commissioned, the carbon credit benefits would increase by generating carbon credits from clean energy generation and waste management projects. The projects registered are eligible for a total period of 30 years.

□

19

Making the People Aware

Effective Communication Model Helped Connect with People in Clean India Mission

The success of any programme or scheme depends on the communication skills of those in charge. A scheme or a plan can be prepared, but its implementation is not that easy. It may require a lot of planning and successful communication with the target audience. For the successful implementation, it must first be ensured that the scheme's benefits reach the beneficiaries. It is a difficult task, but it can be made easy if some details are understood. The main factor that led to the success of Swachh Bharat Abhiyan in Indore was that the people were not only made aware of cleanliness but also developed a feeling in their mind that the campaign was not for the benefit of the people alone but also necessary for the beauty of the city.

We found this task difficult in the initial phase, but we discussed with our team how we could best communicate with the locals and win their support for the sanitation drive. One thing brought to our notice was that the people in

Indore are more educated, and so slogans should be written in English and Hindi, which would increase awareness among the people. The suggestion was fine, but it was not entirely practical. We wanted to target young and educated people, but people in the age group of fifty years and above too were our potential beneficiaries and had to be conveyed to them as well.

After lengthy deliberations, the problem was finally resolved. The slogans were written the way the objectives of Swachh Bharat Abhiyan are written, but their style was changed. Each slogan was given a local flavour. Hindi and English words were used wherever appropriate, but such simple words were used that even an ordinary person could understand easily. For the project's success and to connect more people with it, we used the local dialect as much as possible.

It is easy for everyone to understand the word 'Bhiya'. Brother is also not a big problem as most people understand it, but the problem is that this word does not have that sweetness that can attract people. In such a situation, the address 'Bhiya' was used in place of 'Bhaiya' and 'Brother'. As soon as you speak Bhiya, it automatically dissolves like sugar candy in the ears. Bhiya is so prevalent in Indore that one gets attracted by this word. Similarly, 'kiya' is used in common parlance, but Indoris use the words 'kara' and 'kari' for 'kiya'.

For example, *'Nagar Nigam Kari Pukar, Tailet ne Vapro har Baar'.* In this, the English word 'toilet' has also been used but changed to 'tailet' in the local dialect. Similarly, 'istemal' is the commonly used Hindi equivalent for the word 'use'. But instead of using this word, the word 'vapro' is being used in the local dialect so that more people could connect with the campaign. After reading and listening to this slogan, the consciousness of the local residents awakened, and they realised that they have to use toilets to keep Indore city clean.

Similarly, for advising about the use of toilets, a slogan was made like this—*'Tailet Mein Jo Jaaye, Vere Ghare Bimari Na Aawe'*. Translated in English, it means that by using clean toilets, diseases can also be avoided. The local dialect used by Indoris has been skillfully and intelligently used in this slogan.

In another slogan, the use of vernacular language has made it popular among the people—*'Ni Malam To Hodi Lo, Google Pe Jai Ne Tailet Khoji Lo'*. This simply means that if you do not have the information about the toilet, then there is no need to search much; just Google it. People have been advised and encouraged to use modern means of communication and the Internet in their local language. With these experiments, the city's residents were not bored of slogans as they were so appealing and different from the common slogans. As people love their dialect, awareness was developed about keeping the city clean.

Various measures have been taken to make Indore the best city in the Swachh Bharat Abhiyan. It is clear from this example of the use of local dialect in the slogans that a scheme's objectives can be communicated to the people. Simply writing routine slogans brings dullness. Along with this, some sketches and cartoons and pictures have also been used. These pictures grab people's attention, prompting them to see and read the slogans written on the walls and hoardings and associate with them.

But one cannot expect much change from slogan writing alone. Various precautions have been taken throughout this campaign. As I have mentioned earlier, we obtained a positive result using the local dialect; apart from this, many other things were taken care of. Indore is recognised as a culturally rich and diverse city, so surely our campaign should also be developed in a way that the city's cultural vibrancy could be depicted. For this, we took care of the colour scheme of the pictures made with the slogans. Bright colours were used as Indoris have a particular inclination towards bright colours. When you go to Indore, the colour of their clothes and decoration of homes and shops naturally attracts you. Bright colours give a feeling of zeal for life. Therefore, mostly yellow and blue colours have been used in each slogan and for the pictures used in the background.

In the pictures and the characters used with the slogans, special care has been taken to ensure their faces and clothes reflect the culture of the local people. Men usually wear a turban on the head, hence, the use of turbans in slogans. For the female character too, care has been taken that the woman has a 'pallu' on her head. In Indori culture, women step out of the house only with a pallu on their heads. Some funny characters have been used. For example, a teacher is giving a message to people with a stick in her hand, but in order to make it more attractive, the size of the teacher's glasses has been enlarged. Looking at such pictures brings a smile to the people's faces, and the message is conveyed to them effectively. Call it Indori culture or Malwi culture, Mandana is traditionally quite popular here. Whether it is Teej-festival or celebration, it is a part of life. It is seen as the joy of life. Therefore, an attempt has been made to use Mandana in the posters of the slogan.

Our experiences have been totally different. To make these slogans effective, we undertook a special study of the literary, cultural traditions of Indore. The slogans have been prepared after discussing with the local people. After the slogans were ready, the big problem was where and how to place the posters of the slogan for display. If attractive slogan posters are put up in crowded places, there is an increased risk of accidents. But these posters will have no effect in deserted or less crowded areas.

In such a situation, it was decided that posters should be put up at places like bus stands, markets and public places with stop signs. Buses in Indore have a fixed route, and traffic is not obstructed if the slogan posters were to be put up at these places. Similarly, these posters were put up at the places where people gather to eat and drink to discipline themselves and deposit the garbage at the fixed spots. In this way, people were inspired to make Indore the best city in the Clean India Mission through this communication model. Today, Indore has become famous as the cleanest city, and it has carved a niche for itself by successively retaining this tag.

□

20

People behind this Wonderful Deed

Former Indore Mayor Mrs. Malini Gaud

To accomplish the goal of the Swachh Bharat Mission set by Honourable Prime Minister Shri Narendra Modi, we made every effort in which we were successful. We got the total support of Honourable Chief Minister Shri Shivraj Singh Chauhan in this work, who constantly provided us guidance from time to time and fulfilled our needs.

Whenever I used to see the garbage bins in Indore city, I used to experience a strange pain in my mind on looking at them and the garbage scattered around them with stray animals roaming around the pile of trash. In the year 2015, I was elected as the mayor of Indore city. As soon as I took responsibility as mayor, I first decided that these garbage boxes have to be removed from the city. In 2015, Indore was ranked 150th in cleanliness in the country, while in 2016, it had reached 25th place.

We conducted several campaigns in the city to make the local people aware of cleanliness. How the people of the city ought to make cleanliness their habit was the biggest challenge for us. In order to bring about a radical change in the people's behaviour, we interacted with businessmen, residents, coordinated with many associations like doctors, engineers, schools and colleges, and conducted more than 500 meetings with them. Efforts like the Roko Toko campaign, radio jingle, video films to segregate the wet and dry waste and put it in the garbage vehicle were also fruitful.

In the year 2017, Indore became the cleanest city in the country for the first time. We started using machines for cleaning during day and night. The streets of the city started looking clean and beautiful. In order to increase the greenery and beauty in the city, plantations were done on the central dividers, and attractive flowering plants were planted.

After making Indore the cleanest city in the country, the challenge was even bigger to maintain this spot. The rules of the 2018 Swachh Survekshan were tougher than ever, but we Indoris didn't baulk. We got together; every aspect was understood in detail, and every single point was worked on, and innovations were effected. All these efforts took Indore to a new dimension. A 3R Conference was held in Indore in which delegates from more than 70 countries participated, and the Indore 3R declaration took place. Now we were working on Reduce, Reuse and Refuse. Composting from wet waste, composting dry waste, and now we were segregating and employing rag pickers. Indore stood number one in the year 2018 as well, with innovative ideas like using plastic sheets in road construction, eliminating household waste at home, and making CNG gas from waste. This journey did not stop here and continued like this in 2019 and 2020.

We have made a system by following that we can make Indore number one in cleanliness forever. It was not an easy task for Indore to rank number one for five consecutive times. The credit for this goes to the lakhs of people of Indore, local public representatives, the then Municipal Commissioner Manish Singh, Ashish Singh, all the officers and employees of the Indore Municipal Corporation who extended their valuable contribution in this work.

Indore Municipal Commissioner Pratibha Pal

Indore is called the dream city of Madhya Pradesh. The civic authorities there are witnessing the past memories coming alive with the drain tapping campaign carried out by the Indore Municipal Corporation vigorously throughout the city. The drains have dried up in the west zone of the city. Along with this, wells dug there have started to get filled with water.

After nearly 150 years, bright memories of the past are being brought anew to the new generation; Indore city has experimented every time after winning the title of the cleanest city in the country. The most important thing is that Indore has continuously brought changes in cleanliness every year, and the city makes it an ongoing practice.

This Water Cures Diseases

By the way, the city's municipal corporation has been running a campaign of tapping the drains for the last several months. While running this campaign, it was claimed by the corporation officials that the dirty water flowing in the drains has to be removed from there and has to be again brought into the river as before. The Municipal Corporation has started this work. The task itself was very challenging, but the municipal officials did not back down in meeting this challenge. As a result of this, meaningful signs of this campaign are now visible. In this, the city has set aside Rs. 550 crores to clean the city's drains and rejuvenate the Saraswati River. Funds are being utilised for works like construction of sewerage treatment plant (STP), laying of primary and secondary lines of sewerage, drain-outfall tapping, river front development and beautification. All these works are being done simultaneously, which were earlier planned to be completed in a phased manner.

These works are being done for two to three years, but the municipal corporation has speeded them up to obtain the clean survey and water plus certificate for the last few months. So far, 350 families have tapped 486 domestic outfalls of the Saraswati river at their own expense. This trend will also continue in tapping the outfalls of Kahn River and six drains. The biggest challenge in this is to complete all the ongoing works by November-December because only can they be included in the Swachh survey, and Indore will obtain the water plus certificate.

Things that will Change the Fate of Rivers

Corporation officials say that STPs are being built in the city at the cost of Rs. 280 crores. The primary and secondary sewerage lines are being laid at the cost of Rs. 120 crores. About Rs. 50 crores have been spent on river front development in the 3.9 km long stretch from Karbala bridge to Rambagh bridge. Apart from this, other works, including six drains and outfall tapping, are being done.

Out of 5,600 plus outfalls in the city, 1,400 to 1,500 domestic outfalls have been tapped. This work will be done in a 9.5 km long stretch of Saraswati River from Bijalpur to Krishnapura Bridge with drains and a 9.5 km long stretch of Kahnriver from Tezpur to Krishnapura.

Preparations are on to make Kahn River, Azad Nagar, Bhamori and Jailiya Khal Nala outfall free by November. Azad Nagar STP is set to start on 30 October. The STP of Canal Bhandara has been started from Sunday. Works of about Rs. 500 crores are being carried out for the past two to three years to stop the inflow of dirty water into the rivers and streams of the city, informs Sandeep Soni, Additional Commissioner, Municipal Corporation.

Indore moving towards a World Record

Indore, which has consistently become number one in cleanliness, is now moving towards making a world record. According to Municipal Commissioner Pratibha Pal, the Municipal Corporation is preparing to make a record of segregating six types of garbage from one lakh houses of the city simultaneously. The corporation wants to register this event in the Guinness Book of World Records or Limca Book of Records. However, the pre-recording process is lengthy and will take some time. Municipal Commissioner Pratibha Pal said that this waste is already being taken separately from the houses or institutions in the city, but by organising such an event, the corporation wants to set a unique example before the Ministry of Urban Development. For this, apart from the municipal officers, the NGO team is contacting the people in the resident associations, townships etc., and motivating them to participate in the event.

At present, no city in the country is handling six types of garbage separately. Still, Indore was the first to collect waste like plastic, domestic organic waste, tube lights, bulbs, paint cans, COVID waste, along with the wet-dry waste. The IMC has been using and disposing of these different categories of waste separately. For this, the people of the city are constantly being made aware. By organising programmes in the entire city, people are being informed about the six bin concept.

The municipal commissioner said that garbage like tube lights and domestic organic waste does not emanate from houses every day, so on a single day, at a time, all six types of aggregate waste are being collected from one lakh houses together. Every Saturday and Sunday, the corporation conducts such programmes to spread cleanliness awareness and new messages among the residents. The upcoming event is also linked to that.

The Municipal Corporation is preparing to take some big steps to make the city a smart and safe city. Under the Community Camera Policy, preparations are being made to make it mandatory to install CCTV cameras in commercial properties of size exceeding 1,500 square feet. Under the project, it will be mandatory to install CCTV cameras in all townships, schools, and commercial establishments with more than 100 people's footwork daily.

Corporation officials have said that the Municipal Council has already approved the draft in this regard. It has now been sent to the state government for final approval. It is believed that work on the scheme will be started within two to three months. The corporation has also made preparations to implement some part of the scheme based on private-public partnership, i.e., PPP model. A smart pole has been added to this. By the end of the year, about 60,000 CCTV cameras will be installed across the city, directly connected to the Integrated Control and Command Centre located at the city bus office. After implementing the Community Camera Policy, it is estimated that about Rs. 1 crore will be spent every year on its operation and maintenance. The camera's feed will be made available to the police, RTO or other departments as per the requirement.

Corporation officials said that at present, there are 3,000 CCTV cameras in the city. These cameras have been installed by police, the municipal corporation (smart city company) and the city bus company. The corporation has also decided that on such roads or streets where the crowd is large, but there are no large private markets, the corporation will install cameras on its own as per the requirement. Officials say that at present, the common man does not know which and what type of CCTV cameras should be installed as part of the Community Camera Policy. These standards will be fixed, and it will be announced where, how and how much capacity cameras should be installed.

Bringing Policy in View of the Safety of Women and Elderly

There is a preparation to implement Community Camera Policy to make the city the safest city in the country. Under the project, about 60 thousand cameras are to be installed in the city by the end of 2021. Its basic objective is to provide maximum security to the women and the elderly in the city. The Municipal Corporation will connect 100-200 vendors under the policy, who will supply standard level cameras to the residents. There are about 15,000 such places in the city where cameras will have to be installed. Nevertheless, the corporation is surveying the places to identify more dark areas where it is necessary to install CCTV cameras, prioritising security.

With the commencement of the cleanliness survey in the country, Indore has been achieving a continuous record in the Swachh Bharat Mission for five years in cleanliness, waste management and environmental protection with energy. Indore is all set to be declared as the country's first water plus ranking city soon.

Not only this, but Indore also faced tough competition with Surat, Ahmedabad and Mumbai for the Seven Star Ranking of the Ministry of Urban Development, which is said to be the most difficult in terms of cleanliness. Recently, the survey team has reached Indore to assess the difficult cleanliness parameters of water plus and 7 star city here; based on whose report, Indore can set new records of cleanliness across the country.

Indore Municipal Corporation has been Preparing for Four Years

In fact, preparations were going on in Indore for the last four years to obtain this ranking, which the Ministry of Urban Development will decide. This is the toughest task of waste management and water disposal with cleanliness. This is why the municipal corporation spent more than Rs. 300 crores in four years to prevent residual water impact in the city's major rivers.

For this, the outfall of the city's drains into the rivers was closed on a large scale. The Kahn and Saraswati rivers of the city are flowing with glory as they did in yesteryears.

Planting with Water from Drains

Apart from the rivers, the municipal corporation is filtering the sewer water flowing in the 27 drains of the city and using it for plantation in all the gardens and parks of the city. The water coming out of the houses of all the drains and rivers of the city is purified and connected with a line entailing an expenditure of Rs. 20 crores.

Indore is Stronger than other Cities

The Indore Municipal Corporation has already fulfilled the conditions for the Seven Star ranking. Apart from this, by treating sewage water, the same is already being used in Indore for other needs, including gardening. Not only this, but the problems also arising in the chamber and manholes are resolved only on the App of Indore Municipal Corporation. This type of arrangement currently exists only in Indore. This is the reason why Indore's claim seems more convincing than that of other cities of the country.

Water Plus Protocol

Under the Swachh Bharat Mission, there is now a tough competition between the cities regarding cleanliness and wastewater management, which are in the race to obtain the water plus category. In fact, under the Water Plus protocol, the urban development ministry has set the criteria for treating wastewater from residential houses and commercial establishments of the city before releasing it into the water sources. In this, different marks are fixed for fulfilling different criteria.

These marks are to be given to the respective areas, keeping their water management efforts and experiments in view. In fact, out of the total 1800 marks of Water Plus certification, 1100 marks are fixed for Seven Star Ranking and 700 marks for Water Plus. Indore city became the first Water Plus city when the Government of India announced the competition results in August 2021.

Deployment of Officers on all the Toilets of the City

This time, the focus of the team of cleanliness survey will be public toilets and community toilets constructed by the Municipal Corporation. This is the reason why all the toilets have been glazed. The criteria set for the toilets for cleanliness survey and Seven-Star ranking are already in place here. Wherever there is an apprehension of any shortage, officers have been deployed at all the rest rooms under all the 19 zone offices of the city.

—Ashish Singh

CEO, District Panchayat, Indore 2016

Commissioner, Indore Municipal Corporation

May 2018-2020

The cleanliness drive of Indore has been community-led. We had developed the leadership for its success, after that gradually the same people became the architects of the success of this initiative. To make this successful, the district administration first paid attention to the rural areas and motivators were selected for that.

The motivators were those individuals who could inspire people so that changes could be brought about. First of all, the motivators were selected after which they were given training for five days so that they could inspire people and tell them how we can get rid of open defecation. Provision of incentives was also made for these people so that they could work diligently.

First of all, 5-7 women were grouped to stop open defecation in rural areas. Children were also involved in this entire process. While the women's group used to inspire women, the children's group was given the responsibility of the city so that if they saw anyone, they could immediately stop them from defecating in the open.

Children also gave flowers to those who were found defecating in the open so that they should avoid defecating in the open because of shame. Apart from this, a mike was also used. When the children used to see anyone, they used to speak in the mike. One of the purposes of engaging children was that the elders do not fight with them but listen to them.

During this period, these groups of women and children kept a close watch that no person should defecate in the open. We constantly used to obtain feedback from them so that after assessing the ground situation, if any changes were needed, they could be implemented.

In this period there were many challenges, but the measures taken by the local people helped achieve success easily. It was not easy to change people's habits of the, so it was necessary to keep giving them a message of cleanliness continuously.

In Indore city too, a similar start was made for cleanliness. The success of the rural sector inspired us to implement it in the city as well.

The specialty of the survey conducted annually is that the norms are changed every year. That is why you have to prepare every year afresh to be successful. Earlier there was a survey for three days, but it was changed, and different teams were sent at different times.

The Devguradia Trenching Ground, which is spread over more than 100 acres of land, was such that people did not even like to stand close to it. But when it was decided to remove it, the basic facilities for the landfill site like plant, machinery, road and building were first arranged.

Then the work of separating wet and dry waste was commenced. Earlier, dry waste used to mix with wet waste as it was not separated and kept in the same boxes by the people.

About 13 lakh metric tonnes of old waste lying on the trenching ground was a big problem but was gradually it disposed of using scientific methods. Eight gardens were developed on the ground using old waste soil. Old waste has more odour; so, bio-culture organic matter was added to it so that the foul smell could be controlled. The process of converting waste into compost was also started.

In each ward, about 500 people who pick up garbage were connected to it and they were given work at the trenching ground. They were provided with all the necessary facilities and equipment including training. After this, the automatic machines were used to do the work normally done manually by labourers.

The trenching ground of the city, which became number one in the country in cleanliness, also became the best in compliance with the standards. The trenching ground at Devguradia also got the ISO certificate. This is the first trenching ground in the country which has become ISO. Along with this, an ISO certificate was also obtained for safety and health management.

Indore will be the only city in the country where 100% waste is being disposed of. Such arrangements were made in the trenching ground that first the wet waste is weighed and then it is converted into manure by sending it to the compost plant. Income is also generated by selling this manure for farming and horticulture. Plastic and recycled materials are being separated from dry waste and sent to factories. A thousand rag pickers were involved in this recycling process. The unusable waste coming out of the dry waste began being disposed of by landfill. This whole system was environment- as well as public-friendly.

After this, many such arrangements were made in the city so that not only is the dirt eliminated but the environment too can be protected.

Jhola (bag) banks, utensils banks were all part of this process. You can obtain a bag from Jhola Bank by donating your old clothes. In the same way, you can obtain utensils for use from the utensil bank. Its purpose is to reduce people's use of disposables. It can be obtained from the municipal corporation for any programme or ceremony without paying any fee, but disposables must not be used in the programme.

Door to door collection was also started in Indore city. An IT-driven system was then developed to keep track of vehicles. From this it could also be known how much garbage was picked up. After this, the initiative of cleaning the river drains was also undertaken.

It can be stated that the success of any work cannot be achieved without the cooperation of the stakeholders, politicians, media and administration. Everyone's cooperation has been obtained in this endeavour too and that is why it has proved successful in every way.

The success of Indore shows that money can also be earned by using waste properly. Manure was made from dry waste and money was earned from what was sold.

□

21

Indore's Councillors—The Pride of Indore

If we talk about the cleanliness of Madhya Pradesh's commercial capital Indore, then the prominent role played by the people's representatives have to be mentioned. If a city in a country claims the title of the cleanest city for five consecutive times, then surely it cannot be possible without the cooperation of the people's representatives.

There have been many such councillors in the Indore Municipal Corporation who brought changes in their wards in every way and obtained the cooperation of the people and managed to make the city clean.

One of them is Dilip Sharma, the councillor of Ward 43. Dilip Sharma has occupied the position of a councillor of Indore Municipal Corporation twice. For the first time, Dilip Sharma has been a councillor from ward 45 Geeta Bhawan from 2009 to 2015. For the years 2015 to 2020, he was elected from ward 43 Srinagar Palasia.

The biggest quality of Dilip Sharma is that when awareness was created about cleanliness in Indore, as a public representative, he tried to explain to the people in every way how they can keep their area clean.

Dilip Sharma had said, "This was the beginning of a campaign that the public had never thought of. After the appeal of Prime Minister Narendra Modi, people were acquiring a little understanding of how important cleanliness is. But in a city like Indore, it required a lot of changes."

But after Indore stayed on top for the third time in a row, Dilip Sharma organised a unique event in the city. He organized a 'tiffin party' on Adarsh Road (Greater Kailash Road) under his leadership. Public representatives and common people sat and ate food on the decorated pavement of the road. That day was 25th December 2019, the birthday of former Prime Minister Bharat Ratna (late) Atal Bihari Vajpayee, as well as Christmas. People appreciated this new experiment and brought food from homes and relished it while sitting on the road's sidewalk.

The people involved in the tiffin party said that such roads should be constructed in every ward so that instead of going out for picnics, they could enjoy by the roadside itself. During the tiffin party, people also celebrated the birthday of former Prime Minister Vajpayee by cutting a cake.

Dilip Sharma informed the gathering that Chief Minister Shivraj Singh Chouhan had said that the road should be cleaned and decked up so that people could sit there and eat food. The real message of Shivraj Singh Chouhan was that the roads should be so clean that people should not feel any reluctance to sit there and have food.

Inspired by this, he organised this event on this road.

This road has been built at a cost of Rs.7 crores. Dilip Sharma says that this road holds a special position not only in the state but also the country.

Previously, this road was occupied by handcarts, and encroachment could be seen everywhere. But Dilip Sharma first convinced vendors in such a manner that they vacated without any protest.

Dilip Sharma wants every road in the city to be like that. The speciality of this road is that the members of the Standing Committee of Parliament too have come and seen it.

There is also a wall of goodness on this road, where people come and leave the goods and their belongings for those who need them. The needy can pick up the goods from here. Apart from this, Dilip Sharma has done another great work; he built a wall of education on this road. Its speciality is that anyone can come here and donate old books for the use of someone in need.

The objective of this initiative is to provide the means of education to the children. A lattice room has been built to prevent misuse of the books kept there. One person has been appointed to maintain the details of the book donor and the recipient. Apart from this, people can also submit the names and necessary of unavailable books in a box. People can also donate books, copies, pencils, and other educational material as they prefer.

With the help of people, Dilip Sharma has so far made books worth 25 thousand rupees available to the children.

The local people have given a very positive response to this initiative. They say it is good and it should be like this in every city in the country.

Dilip Sharma says that his endeavour is that children take books from here and, after reading it, when they aare no longer needed, return the books to the same place so that other children can use them. Along with this road, the wall of education initiated by Dilip Sharma is also being praised across the country. Through the wall of education, many people are coming forward to help so that the unprivileged children can get an education.

Apart from this, Dilip Sharma has also built a food ATM on this road, where anyone can bring food and the needy or the hungry one can take food from there.

Dilip Sharma says that every citizen of Indore city is our own, and we must help the needy people.

However, Dilip Sharma says that it is not easy to keep your ward and road clean in this way. They have to give 2-4 hours every day to maintain its cleanliness. If there is even the slightest dirt, they have to immediately call water tankers from the Municipal Corporation and clean it. It's not all that easy. However, he believes that people have incorporated the habit of cleanliness and hygiene into their life.

He said that even if someone eats chocolate here, he does not throw the wrapper on the road, but he first finds a dustbin to put it in.

Dilip Sharma said that he has got works worth up to Rs 30 crores done in his ward. There are 24 gardens in his area, and every garden is unique in its own way. All kinds of facilities are available in the garden. This garden is a better place to spend time with children as well as for the elderly.

Dilip Sharma says that cleanliness has now become a habit of the city. If someone throws the garbage, the people look at it with disgust, making the offender conscious of his wrongdoing.

Rachna Tyagi, who lives in the area, says it is a different place in itself, where people also get comfortable. If the environment is clean, you feel better from the inside, which is a special thing. She says the clean environment in our city makes us prouder.

Dilip Sharma says that the garbage vehicle comes twice in the area, and any garbage in the dustbin on the roadside here is picked up and taken away.

Santosh Gaur has also done similar works regarding cleanliness. Councillor Santosh Gaur's, Ward 12 of Indore was known as a backward and slum area. But the cleanliness campaign changed the face of this area as well. Even if it rained up to only 2 inches in this settlement, the whole area would get inundated. The impact of rainwater used to be such that the people living in the area had to struggle for six months till the time of Diwali.

Santosh Gaur rid the area of this problem. The challenges before them were no less because there were poor and less educated people in the area, and it was equally difficult to explain the benefits of anything to them.

Santosh Gaur said, "Due to the lack of education in the area, there was also a lack of awareness among the people. But despite that, every effort was made to change the picture of the area."

At the same time, Deepak Jain, councillor of Ward No. 6 of Indore, also describes the cleanliness campaign of Indore as a campaign that has given a different identity to the city.

He said that there were two big problems in his area; one was removing the already existing garbage boxes, which itself was littering the areas, and the other was the problem of transporting the cows out of the city.

Door to door garbage collection was to be done after removing the garbage boxes. Still, it was not easy to change people's habits, so many programmes were organised for awareness so that folks could understand its importance. Dustbins were given to people so that they could keep dry and wet waste separately. These dustbins were not given to them for free; they were charged a fee to make them understand their importance. For this, half the money was taken from the institutions.

At the same time, he said that people would feed one *roti* to the cow every day in Hindu society, but when the cows were transported out of the city, this ritual was interrupted and caused uneasiness among many. For this reason, Deepak Jain started the Gau Grass service vehicle for the first time in Indore city.

Through this, pieces of bread were collected from every household, and were donated to cowsheds to be fed to the cows.

Deepak Jain, who has been a councillor since 2015 in this ward of about 45,000, says that his ward has a very dense population, so the challenges were also more.

There is a very old temple in this ward, which is about 250-300 years old, a pilgrimage route is being prepared for it, and along with this, a pilgrimage gate is also being built.

In this ward, Janata Clinic was also started, in which check-ups are done for only 10 rupees. Its speciality is that apart from this, no fee is charged for the medicine, no matter how expensive it may be.

Deepak Jain also organised the first employment fair in his area, in which 45 companies participated and handed out about 170 appointment letters in a single day.

Deepak Jain says that he got the inspiration to do all this after the cleanliness campaign of Indore city led it to bag the number one place in the country.

In Indore, the local leaders were the councillors, and they acquired their inspiration from the city's cleanliness campaign. The completive environment that was created amongst the councillors to make their ward the cleanest ward made the city inch towards greater cleanliness.

□

22

What other Cities can Learn from Indore

Indore has registered its presence as a winner in the entire country not once but repeatedly in cleanliness. Surely, the success of Indore belongs to the whole of Indore, not to one person or administration. Indore's residents understood the importance of cleanliness and pledged to clean their own houses, neighbourhoods, and city and fulfilled the resolution. If I look back, I find it hard to believe that such a phenomenal change has occurred in the lifestyles of the people of Indore in such a short time. The work done by me as an officer of the Indian Administrative Service gives me inner satisfaction. But more than that, the residents of Indore supported me and encouraged me.

When Indore was included in the competition for the cleanest city in the country, it was a big challenge, but the people of Indore have a great passion for their city, which makes them different from others. Perhaps this was the biggest reason that when clean cities were rated in the country for the first time, Indore was number one.

After this, Indore has retained its title year after year. One thing to notice here is that year after year, the terms of the clean city campaign became more and more difficult. But Indore overcame all those challenges as if the people knew beforehand that they would have to face these challenges to make their city the country's cleanest city.

Even after my successful tenure in Indore, this campaign of cleanliness did not cease. The administration and the municipal corporation are working with the same zeal and enthusiasm with the cooperation of the residents in making Indore always clean. My experience says that once you set a standard, you become certain of the result. During my tenure as a collector in Indore, I set some standards to make it the cleanest city in the country. Work continued even after my transfer from Indore, and those standards were made the basis for carrying forward the work. On the orders of the government, I was assigned another responsibility, and had to fulfil it, but my heart remained in Indore. Even today, Indore remains in my mind. It may not be so difficult to make a city clean and bag the top place, but it is challenging to retain the number one place and attain the tag of the country's cleanest city continually and repeatedly.

I am happy that the most capable officers are taking our dreams forward. Local political leaders have also fully supported us and contributed to our success. Without their cooperation, it would have been impossible to complete this mission.

The effort and initiative taken by the Government of India to conduct the sanitation and cleanliness survey to foster a spirit of healthy competition among towns and cities and motivate everyone is unique. Even after 70 years of independence, we have never been aware of cleanliness. Cleanliness in our way of life was limited to our homes and courtyards only. We had earlier never been sensitive about the cleanliness of our neighbourhoods and the city. The consequence of this was that we continued to suffer from many unwanted diseases due to unsanitary conditions. The filth and dirty surroundings caused many physical diseases; they also made the mind sick.

The Government Campaign Opened our Eyes

In the last five years, this campaign of the Government of India has opened our eyes. We are starting to become aware of the benefits of making our cities clean. We are beginning to understand our responsibility. Cleanliness has been included in our life's priorities. Indore is the leader among clean cities; there are many reasons behind it, but the cities that did not figure in the list of cleanest cities or were low in rating have also done better. There are many reasons those cities were not included in the top ratings. All those reasons should be considered, and it should be debated how Indore became a role model defining a clean city.

Indore is a role model in cleanliness not because it has been consistently rated and counted among the cleanest cities in the country, but because people of Indore have a sense of belongingness for their city as they consider the city as their own. Indorians felt that they could create a better and clean city with a little effort, a little help, and a little caution. Now when I talk of Indore, we should know that Indore is a historic city. It is a city of cultural and literary significance.

'Roko-Toko' Campaign Helped Change People's Habits

Popularly known as Mini Bombay, Indore is a large commercial centre, and it is estimated that daily traffic to Indore from other places of the country is highest compared to other cities of Madhya Pradesh. From this point of view, becoming a clean city was a big challenge for Indore. But the 'Roko-Toko' campaign gave life to Indore. It proved a game-changer in helping Indore become the cleanest city. 'Roko-Toko' focused on some identified negative behaviours among the people. People of the city or those coming from outside the city were made aware and responsible for maintaining sanitation. This trick of maintaining cleanliness changed the picture of Indore city gradually, and people stopped littering on the streets unnoticed by others. The garbage began to be dumped in the dustbins kept at the designated places.

You must have experienced that the people's opinion about the municipal corporation or municipality of their city is usually not good. People feel that those employed in such corporations only work for namesake. They do not clean the city properly and with earnestness. People had the same mindset about the Indore Municipal Corporation. But today, the role of Indore Municipal Corporation is most important in making Indore clean. From sanitation workers to top officials, they are busy in their work as they all consider them responsible and accountable in this Swachh Bharat Mission.

Limited Budget was a Problem

A city's budget is allocated to the municipality or municipal corporation at the government level, depending on the city's population. With this often limited budget, all the works of the civic body are completed. It has been observed that most of the time, financial constraints are there, and many tasks remain incomplete even though they may be necessary or in people's interest. Things were no different in the matter of cleanliness. Here also, the city faced a dearth of funds.

A strategy was prepared for this. Collecting garbage from homes was a big task. The challenge was how to complete this work in the absence of vehicles. But acting on a good suggestion, the unused vehicles stranded in the garage were repaired at a nominal cost and put to work.

Shortage of Sanitation Workers

There was a shortage of sanitation workers, but the system was made smooth by employing daily wage workers. Another experience of mine is that when any innovation takes place, local politicians intervene. It is a bit difficult to get them to agree and complete the task with their cooperation. But Indore is completely different in this case. There is no political interference in works that enhance the prestige of the city. In fact, politicians extended their cooperation to make Indore clean.

This sense of belonging was so widespread that the complaints of even well-to-do and influential people of the city were ignored if they tried to create hurdles in the sanitation works. This made the work easy and simple. When we boosted the morale of the people involved in the cleanliness campaign, the situation became so pleasant that if one employee fell ill or was not able to work due to some reason, then another employee used to come forward and take the responsibility so that the work did not suffer.

There Used to be Heaps of Garbage in Night Markets

Indore is a big commercial city, and the food habits here are completely different from other cities. As an outcome, the city produces a lot of garbage. But if you find a solution to a problem and implement it, the problem ceases to exist. Be it Sarafa or 56 Dukan, an adequate number of dustbins have been provided everywhere. People were advised to dispose of garbage in the dustbins after eating. Simultaneously, as soon as the market started, the sanitation staff of the corporation was deployed. They kept constantly cleaning till dawn. The garbage vehicles of the corporation were continuously deployed at these places.

These measures prevented the public from disposing of used cutlery and leftover food in the dustbin. My experience is that before the Swachch Bharat Abhiyan, these night markets of Indore used to be full of filth by late night. Today, the picture has totally changed and the habits of the people as well.

Polythene was a Big Problem

People were motivated to dump garbage in dustbins, and the sanitation workers kept doing their work with full vigour, but this was not enough. Polythene and huge piles of papers were big problems, and we had to deal with them. These things were challenging for Swachch Indore too. However, we found a solution for this as well. We inspired shop owners to use utensils instead of use and throwaway plates and polythene. Initially, the shopkeepers did not like our suggestion, but they agreed with us with a little persuasion and imposition of symbolic penalty.

After some time, feedback was received from these shopkeepers that by using utensils, they were cooperating in the clean Indore mission and also benefitting financially. This feedback was unexpected. We did not even think about it. It was like killing two birds with a single stone. In this way, we successfully completed a most challenging task as the night markets used to produce maximum filth, but we made them spick and span.

Similarly, the concept of bag bank was started. The use of the cloth bags in place of polythene was emphasised in collaboration with the voluntary organisations of the city. Today, cloth bags are seen instead of plastic bags in the hands of the Indoris.

Challenge of Disposing of Garbage

A big challenge now was how to dispose of the garbage. Garbage collection was being done, and it was dumped in a remote and isolated part of the city. The pile of garbage became huge in no time, and soon there was a mountain of garbage. A solution was also found for this. The work of making organic manure from waste was done. After making organic fertiliser from the waste, it was made available in the market at affordable prices for the common people's needs. Along with this, a garden was made at the same place where many kinds of saplings were planted, which also bore fruit. Today they are also being sold because the fruits have been grown without using any chemicals.

Many big companies collaborated by setting up their own plants to dispose of waste to boost these efforts. In return for this work, the companies provided financial support to the corporation and the district administration. Gradually, we were ahead in the rating of Swachh Bharat Mission. Now the lifestyle of Indore's people had changed.

To make the entire city educated and aware, slogans associated with interesting and nostalgic memories were written all over the city. Movies are popular among all sections of society, so posters of such films were selected, giving a message in terms of cleanliness to society. A sufficient number of toilets were constructed in the city, but oftentimes, people could not use them due to lack of information. In such a situation, these toilets were added through Google App, and people were made aware. This was a different type of initiative but was very important for Swachch Indore. Slogans were written in the local language so that people could connect directly and quickly.

Media's Role

The biggest responsibility in making Indore clean was of the media. Everyone positively supported the district administration and the municipal corporation. The media fully supported the initiatives being taken towards making Swachch Indore. News about innovations was prominently published. The cooperation of the media was also that they drew the attention of the administration to areas where additional work was required. Web channels along with FM radio and local television channels also took positive initiatives for Swachch Indore. Municipal corporations and administration made residents aware with the cooperation of media. Voluntary organisations have contributed a lot in completing the picture of Swachh Indore. They helped by organising street plays, film screenings and varied experiments.

The innovations made by Indore, which won the title of Clean City in the Swachh Bharat Mission, need to be implemented across the country as a role model. It is true that every city has different tastes and behaviour, but every part of the country can be clean if some of the efforts and experiments that Indore has made are also replicated at other places.

My suggestions in this context are as follows:

A sense of belongingness should be developed among the residents of their city. For this, organise workshops and tell people that only with their support can their city attain the status of a clean city.

The residents of a city should be divided into three classes. For example, the first category belongs to people related to administration, education and health. The second category should be people interested in social and cultural activities, and the third should be of the lower middle class or slum dwellers. Create awareness campaign strategies for the three classes.

To prevent the use of polythene, the emphasis should be on using utensils and cloth bags.

Strategies should be made, and private companies should be contracted to make manure by collecting garbage.

Those who dump garbage in the open should be strictly advised but not punished.

Groups of youths should be formed, and they should carry out awareness campaigns in their own way in their own localities.

If possible, clean up the locality by forming a group and hand over the garbage to the corporation's garbage vehicle when it arrives. One thing to be kept in mind is to keep wet and dry waste separately so that it would be easier to make compost.

Other plans can be made according to the likes and dislikes of your city, which will lead to success in conducting the Clean City Campaign.

Coordinate with local media and seek their cooperation. Radio, television, web channels and newspapers are helpful in this matter.

Support can also be taken from local leaders in this regard, and they should be requested that no matter how influential a person is, their voice should not rise above our actions. For this, it is necessary that you inform the leaders in advance about the things so that the work is not obstructed.

□

Conclusion

The story of Indore is worth emulating by many other cities. Already many cities got inspired by the success of Indore and have started making their cities clean. This story of Indore is what every citizen in Indian Cities is aspiring for. This is new India. Indore has shown the way. Every city has to be clean and livable. With the Covid pandemic creating a havoc, a much-needed awareness is being felt towards cleanliness and healthy lifestyle. Such a kind of healthy lifestyle is possible only through cleanliness. Each of every citizen has to feel that personal hygiene will alone lead to well being and community healthiness. Such a healthy environment will alone lead to cities being neat and clean and devoid of vector borne diseases of viral infections.

Just imagine cities without cleanliness. What would have been the extent of damage to lives without awareness of cleanliness? Indore city has been fortunate to have citizens who are well aware of cleanliness. This helped them to get over from the pandemic very easily. The air quality is one of the most important issues that urban areas are worried about. How can the air quality improve in the cities? This is again an issue pertaining to cleanliness.

Apart from cleanliness a good number of decisions have to be taken to improve the air quality like reduction of carbon emission, increase green coverage.

With citizens being aware of cleanliness, there is an increased awareness about non-usage of plastic, reuse of articles etc. So, an informed and aware citizen is what cities need. Indore has shown the right direction for other cities. Whilst improving the cleanliness of the cities, there is an emerging much informed citizenry as well. This will make cities much more livable and purer.

□□□